NOW THAT I'M A MOTHER... WHAT DO I DO FOR ME?

NOW THAT I'M A MOTHER... WHAT DO I DO FOR ME?

Susan Meilach Seligman

Contemporary Books, Inc.
Chicago

Library of Congress Cataloging in Publication Data

Seligman, Susan Meilach.
Now that I'm a mother, what do I do for me?

Bibliography: p.
Includes index.
1. Mothers. I. Title.
HQ759.S45 306.8′7 80-65932
ISBN 0-8092-7156-7
ISBN 0-8092-7155-9 (pbk.)

Published by Contemporary Books, Inc.
180 North Michigan Avenue, Chicago, Illinois 60601
Manufactured in the United States of America
Library of Congress Catalog Card Number: 80-65932
International Standard Book Number: 0-8092-7156-7 (cloth)
0-8092-7155-9 (paper)

Published simultaneously in Canada by
Beaverbooks
953 Dillingham Road
Pickering, Ontario L1W 1Z7
Canada

For
Richard,
Jordan,
and Adam

Happiness, joy, and pleasure are simply the by-products of day-to-day living. They rise to the surface as you are involved in creative, fulfilling, and satisfying days.

—JEAN RAY LAURY
Designer, Author, Mother

Contents

Preface

When my oldest son Jordan was twenty months old, a time when children begin their initial break for independence, I sensed the rumblings of a new kind of frustration within myself. For the past year and a half, I had spent most of my energy nurturing this child. I had had flings with various crafts, had taken jazz dancing and slimnastics classes to keep busy. Each day I felt a growing sense of stagnation. I was occupying my time. Fine. But I wasn't doing anything particularly satisfying. Where was my life headed?

Before Jordan was born, I had worked in the advertising and public relations field. I never really enjoyed the jobs that I held. My degree was in communications. What could I do with that now?

I researched career information at the library. I scoured the bookstores for any volumes or chapters that might inspire me about how to deal with restructuring my life, coupled with the responsibility of my child. There were scores of books about child care, but little information was available on the care of mothers. Funny, I thought; so much is written on the nurturing of the child. Who nurtures the mothers? All the books missed this major point. Happy, well-adjusted children are probably the result of happy, well-adjusted mothers. Does anyone care about the mothers?

I care.

I care because I know what it feels like to have a first baby away from family; to watch your husband go off to the challenges of his work and find yourself at home, alone, with little preparation for the major change in your life. I know what it feels like to tick off your accomplishments for the day as a trek to the grocery store or the cleaner or perhaps, for a highlight, two hours in the pediatrician's waiting room with a sick child. And, I know the frustration of looking ahead to more and more days and months of the same, not knowing what you really want out of life.

I also know the feeling of finding something to do that you really enjoy, that will make each day exciting, that will make being a woman, a mother, a person, in today's world, a most wonderful time of your life.

I am twenty-nine years old. I have two sons: Jordan is three and a half, and Adam is six months old. I love being a mother. However, I know that foremost I am a person. For me to be a good mother, I must be happy with myself as a person. When my days are stimulated, my mothering is filled with joy.

What caused this turnabout in my life? I had the idea to write this book. Each day I was anxious to get to my typewriter. I worked during Jordan's afternoon nap. When he awoke, it was fun to be with him, because each day, I had accomplished something for myself. I respected myself. I believed strongly in what I was doing. I felt great.

It has not been the easiest year of my life, but it was certainly a full year. During the same month that my publisher contracted to write the book (he had seen only sample chapters) I found out that I was pregnant with my second child. I had a rough pregnancy. At the same time, my husband had to make several major career decisions. In my eighth month of pregnancy, we moved from the Washington, D.C., area to Albuquerque, New Mexico. My son Adam was born two weeks later, three and a half weeks early, before our furniture had even arrived from Washington.

Throughout this period of upheaval and turmoil one thing constantly held me together—writing this book. No matter how hectic my schedule, regardless of the disappointments, the decisions, and the frustrations of this year, I felt I was writing to a friend, sharing much of my life with you. I was excited every time I received a new bit of information. I couldn't wait to write you, tell you, hoping it would ultimately help you in some way.

I feel as if I have talked to you daily, experienced so much of this last year with you. In a way, I am sad that the book is finished. It is the feeling you have when you finish reading a good novel. You have become so involved with a character that you miss her when the book is over. I will miss sharing with you.

There is a special bond between us, between all mothers. We must support each other, because few others will. Even the women's movement seems to forget we are people with definite and individualistic needs.

If you have a moment, after you have read the book, drop me a note in care of my publisher. I'd love to hear from you. Let me know what special programs for mothers are available in your city, or what you wish there would be. If you just need a friend to write to, to share feelings about mothering, please write. I understand!

Susan Meilach Seligman
Albuquerque, New Mexico
February, 1980

Acknowledgments

I would like to thank the many, many mothers who participated in interviews and discussion groups. Where would we be without each other?

Thanks to Beverly Greenfeig of the University of Maryland Counseling Center, and to Linda Tossman, director of volunteers at New Phase: A Career Readiness Center in Rockville, Maryland. To the directors of the Fund for the Improvement of Post Secondary Education and the Project on the Status and Education of Women of the Association of American Colleges, appreciation for your tremendous information.

To Davida Scher, Barbara Mandel, Phyliss Ginsberg, Sue Anne Copeland, Ruth Lorber, and Jill Miller, thanks for your support during the last year.

To my mother, Dona Z. Meilach, my constant source of inspiration, my "editor," and my best friend, how can I thank you enough? To my father, Melvin M. Meilach, thanks for all you've done for me, for us, in so many ways.

To my husband, Richard, my heartfelt thanks for your patience, your suggestions, your encouragement, your love, and your friendship—and for making me a mother!

NOW THAT I'M A MOTHER... WHAT DO I DO FOR ME?

PART I

DISCOVERING YOU! A PERSON *AND* A MOTHER

1

A New Outlook on Motherhood

You peer into the crib. You watch the new life before you sleeping ever so soundly. Your beautiful new baby, the life that you brought into this world. Strange new emotions flood through your body. You feel beautiful, radiant—and frightened.

As you sort through the baby gifts, the rattles, the diapers, the many accouterments that surround this new life, are you sorting out how *your* life fits into this picture? Your life as a person as well as a mother?

Have you asked, "What will my life be like now? How will I integrate this tiny, precious human being into my life as a person, into our lives as a couple, and become a family? The responsibility seems so overwhelming. Will I ever have tim[e] for myself again, or will the real me be subservient to th[e] helpless being in that crib?" I'm sure these thoughts fla[sh] through the mind of every woman in the world as she watc[h] her infant sleep. We realize there is no turning back. We mourn for the loss of a former life. A loss of freedom.

Put the mourner's cloth away. There's no time to grieve for that former life. We raise a toast to celebrate a new life—*your* life as a person, a mother, a woman. A life open to *NEW!* New horizons. New thoughts. New feelings, ideas, creativity. Today you will look in the mirror and ask yourself, "Now that I'm a mother, what do I do for *me*?"

Gone are the days when mothers spent each minute doting on every movement of their child, attending to every speck of dust on their furniture, every elaborate meal for their families. Today mothers are people first; they are entitled to the same freedoms and growth to which every other person is entitled. The word *housewife* should be stricken from the English language. Who today feels married to a home? How can a pine-scented bathroom fulfill anyone's idea of a complete day?

Will you ever have time to begin to think of yourself as a person?

The answer is a resounding yes!

Accept the first three months of motherhood as a hazing period. Acccept the fact that you have to go through it. This time is a training period. An apprenticeship. An internship. At the three- or four-month mark, your baby should be sleeping through the night, taking regular naps, and rewarding you for your hard work with the smiles, chortles, and recognition that make it all worthwhile.

When your baby reaches this milestone, your life will begin
eel ordered. Usually your baby will take a morning nap for
an hour and a half and an afternoon nap of perhaps
three hours. That leaves you three to four hours each
you can call completely your own.

ll you do with that time? Clean? Cook? Or discover
otential? Your answers to this important question
fference in your life as a person.

written that once you have a child you are
home, concerned only with domesticity. This

is a time in your life when you should think of your options as completely open. You have time to discover your inner self, what you'd really like to do. Time to dig deep and unearth who you are, where you're going. Time to experiment with life, try new things. The saying, "Today is the first day of the rest of your life" will never be truer than it is now. There are so many options open to women today. Let's begin to celebrate your new life together!

2

The Postpartum Rainbow

I hereby make a formal protest against the phrase *postpartum blues*. How dare anyone take all of the emotional ups and downs of a major experience in one's life and lump them together in one broad phrase—and a negative one at that! If ore physicians, hospital personnel, and childbirth educators uld take as much time giving support to parents after their 's birth as before, the word *blues* might become obsolete.

ATIONS VS. REALITY

or events in our lives are surrounded by expecta- never fulfilled. Weddings, parties, graduation, l experience, a new job, moving—all are events to and envision in a specific way, but which out as we had anticipated. The same goes the first few months that follow. So much emphasis is put on the actual delivery as the greatest emotional experience in one's life. We see films of women who have gone through twenty hours of LaMaze breathing and have the smiles of madonnas on their faces when the baby arrives. I felt after fifteen hours of labor that what was going on in the mirror above me was another LaMaze movie and I was an observer in someone else's delivery. I couldn't believe it was really happening to me. I had pictured wanting to hold and love the baby, but somehow, the great maternal response that I had always expected wasn't there. Hell, I was tired, sore, and frankly, out of it!

And then those first three months! There is no joy in getting up at two o'clock every morning. A colicky baby isn't one's picture of the Gerber child cooing and gurgling from a million-dollar nursery and being cuddled by a beautiful mother in a designer negligee. Yes, engorged breasts hurt. Making formula every day gets old fast. A week's worth of diaper service diapers does smell, and maybe you weren't aware that stools from breastfed babies tend to leak out of a disposable diaper all over your leg. You're exhausted, lonely. The new responsibility seems overwhelming. The sudden loss of freedom and lifestyle is frightening.

But there is joy in an infant suckling from your breast, growing ever so quickly, nourished only from your body. There is joy in watching a newborn sleep so peacefully in his crib. And to say nothing of the real miracle—that you created this wonder inside your body, and the months of watching your stomach grow produced a living, breathing, beautiful human being.

All of these emotions, joyful and not so joyful, will weave a pattern in the next few months that you will probably never forget. The last thing you need when you are feeling down is for someone to say, "Oh, you just have the baby blues!" Sorry, you have real concerns, fears, and joys, and the thing that you need most is support, support from other mothers just like you.

MOTHERS' SUPPORT GROUPS

New mothers are quickly recognizing that the strongest support comes from their own ranks. So many women have their first babies away from their families that friends take on this traditional role. Even strangers are often more supportive than a relative who says, "Well, in my day . . ." Informal get-togethers, coffees, discussion groups, lectures, and other general support groups have mushroomed throughout the country.

You can find out about many of these support groups through a LaMaze instructor. My friend Sue Anne, who lives in a suburb of Chicago, was delighted with a pamphlet she received entitled *No One Ever Told Us!* The pamphlet described some of the normal feelings that mothers have after giving birth. It also included a bibliography of books about child care, breastfeeding, nutrition, education and discipline, and books for mom. A reference sheet listed numbers and services of the poison control center, visiting nurses association, La Leche League, parental stress hotline, Caesarean section support group, mother and child groups, baby-sitting services, and other numbers and information for new mothers.

"A woman came to our last LaMaze class and we filled out cards with our names and addresses," Sue Anne related. "We were called about a month after our approximate due dates and invited to a coffee meeting made up of new mothers. It was wonderful to get together with women for sharing and comparing."

The International Childbirth Education Association is involved with some of these support groups. If you are unable to find out about any in your area, write to the International Childbirth Education Association, Inc., P.O. Box 20852, Milwaukee, WI 53220. They will direct you to your local or regional representative.

No one in the world can help you with your special problems as well as someone who has gone through it before or someone who is experiencing the same feelings. You may find yourself crying during the day for no major reason. Little things can set you off. You may feel totally disoriented. You may have been a completely organized person; now you can never find your keys or glasses when you're ready to go out the door. You feel that your husband isn't taking enough responsibility for the baby. Your whole day seems to go from feeding to feeding to shopping to cleaning to going to bed. You find you can't speak a coherent sentence. All of these emotions are synonymous with having a new baby. Some feelings are caused by hormonal changes that make you an emotional wreck. Others occur because you are tired, unsure of your new role, and perhaps frustrated because you can't do all of the things you thought you could do and wanted to do.

We all overprepare for the birth of our first child, reading every book and forming a zillion preconceived ideas and theories on how things are going to be. When we are actually mothers, faced with the baby every day, our plans and ideas quickly change and adapt. I often chuckle to myself when I hear women in their ninth month of pregnancy laying out absolutes for their first weeks after leaving the hospital. When the baby comes, so much of what they had expected doesn't happen the way it was planned. I know; it happened to me—to all of us.

OVERCOMING THOSE BLUES

It is essential to get plenty of rest during this postpartum period. Forget the housework. Your mental health is more important than a clean floor. When you are well rested, it is easier to deal rationally with the rapid changes that are happening in your life.

During the first few weeks, don't make elaborate plans for your days. Be content with accomplishing the basics and you won't feel frustrated. Set simple daily goals such as a walk with the baby after lunch, trying a new recipe, or visiting a friend. Keep activities simple and enjoyable and do more as you feel up to it. Pamper yourself as much as possible. The first three months are the hardest. Get through them the most enjoyable way you can.

The postpartum rainbow is made up of many colors, and various shades of each. If you think only "blue," you are limiting your vision of what the postpartum period can be. Some women sit around waiting for "the depression" to hit them, expecting but never experiencing it. Some may have only a touch of the blues in an otherwise bright spectrum.

A friend of ours with a newborn baby phoned recently. She sounded miserable. She had been home alone for several days since her husband was out of town. The baby cried all day and wouldn't sleep. She was bored with being home. Depressed. Doesn't everyone have that feeling once in a while? Richard and I calmed her, then sang a barroom ditty in perfect disharmony over the phone to cheer her. That was the end of her blues.

There are, of course, some women who feel blue for days, even weeks. If they recognize it, talk out their feelings with women in the same situation, they may minimize postpartum problems and eliminate them quickly.

FEELING GREAT

Feeling and looking good is a way to pick a sunny color from the postpartum rainbow. When my friend Davida told me it took her three months to feel normal again, I didn't believe it would take me that long. I felt fine only a few weeks after Jordan was born. She was right. When Jordan began to sleep from six to six, with a fairly regular nap schedule, my life took on a new sense of order. No matter how great I thought I had felt before, the end of that three-month period marked a new beginning and a freedom in my life.

Part of beating the blues battle during this postpartum time, is to look and feel great. First, be aware that you aren't going to get into your prepregnancy jeans until after three to four weeks following your baby's birth. Don't even try to squeeze into them until that time. It may be depressing to have to wear those maternity jeans you swore you never wanted to see again, but comfort is important. Your body does look better than it did a few weeks ago; it just needs a little more time. Also, be warned that once you do get back into your clothes, they may not fit exactly as they did before, because your body has taken on more womanly curves. It's not so terrible. Instead of wearing a junior 9, now you may need a 10. Didn't the junior label read 9-10 anyway?

What about your hair? Your makeup? Could you stand a new look? Buy a fashion magazine and study the current styles. Make an appointment to get a good haircut and styling. Stop at a cosmetic counter. Are your makeup shades out of date? If you buy only a new lipstick or an eye shadow, it will brighten your day.

Dress up and look good for yourself. It's easy to get up every day, pull on a pair of jeans and a T-shirt and not do much about your appearance. When I went to a shopping mall, I always wondered why I looked like something the cat dragged in. There were many mothers with small children who looked stunning. The difference was in attitude. I never considered putting on makeup or caring how I looked to run to a mall. But these mothers in nicer jeans or slacks, makeup, stylish hairdos, and pretty jewelry were really put together! That was the time I realized that when I was working I did my hair, applied makeup, and wore a well-coordinated outfit. Mothering is my job now. Why do I have to look like I'm ready to paint the fence every day, when I can look and feel good with just a little effort?

Buy one casual outfit that you can put on to look great on a Tuesday if you feel like it. Don't save everything nice to wear only when you go out. Yes, I know you don't want the baby to spit up on something new and nice, but if it's washable, so what? Try a wraparound skirt for a change, a comfortable dress, washable tailored slacks. Just as your husband gets tired of dressing up for the office every day, you'll need a change from your jeans and sweater every once in a while for you.

EXERCISING FOR A NEW YOU

Nutrition and exercise are an important part of the new you. No, I'm not going to include one of those nutrition charts with the four basic food groups for you to skim. It is essential for you to eat well-balanced meals, especially if you are nursing. You know that, right? Lay off the junk food. No lectures from me; just do it!

Begin your exercise routine when you get home from the hospital. Start with stretching and toning routines and gradually progress to more strenuous exercises. About three weeks postpartum, when the bleeding subsides, you can really begin working on getting yourself back into shape.

OK, I know you hate to exercise. Standing in a room counting twenty-five sit-ups isn't fun. How can it be? How about a little music? Find a record or tape that gets you moving. Turn on the radio. Develop an exercise routine that is fun, not work. If you have a leotard, put it on; you'll feel good! My favorite was a tape by Herbie Hancock, "Watermelon Man." To this day, whenever I hear it, I start moving!

There are many terrific new ways to exercise that shed inches and are fun, too. Try Jazzercising. It's a marvelous way to exercise using modern dance steps. Or aerobic dancing. Tap and ballet are also fun. Belly dancing can do wonders for your tummy, and your marriage! You may enjoy yoga, a wonderful way to trim your body and relax as well. You don't have to touch your toes ten times in a row to slim down.

Be aware of your back. Posture is very important. You'll notice how quickly you'll fall into bad back habits. Carrying your baby on one hip is a sure way to develop a bad back. Stooping to pick up children's toys and other objects without bending your knees can also lead to problems. And, inevitably, you will be holding your child as he gets bigger, putting more and more cricks in your back. Take a good look at your daily routine and concentrate on ways to be good to your back. You'll feel better for it!

3

On Being at Home

Suddenly you are at home. A homemaker. Do these words conjure up thoughts of soap operas, quiz shows, fuzzy pink slippers, and a sparkling commode? What a vision of today's new mother! Being at home is not a limiting proposition. It can be the most expanding and exhilarating time of your life.

NEW DIRECTIONS

Being at home today offers a wonderful time to sit back and explore your thoughts, your feelings, your goals, and your environment. You have been programmed for so long—school, job, career, someone else's schedule, society's formula for success. You now have time to do whatever you have been longing to try—maybe needlepoint, going back to school, taking photography classes, writing poetry, looking into a new career, decorating your home.

Being at home is a time to get in touch with yourself, to slowly consider options that are open to you for the rest of your life. New directions! New interests! New feelings! A time to celebrate yourself!

Perhaps you enjoyed dance while you were in school. Why not take a ballet class? A jazz dance class? Try tap? Or, attend a dance program.?

Are you interested in foreign travel? Now you have the time to read extensively about any area. You can study the language, or take a cooking class in that country's cuisine. Often, your own interest will motivate you to get more out of a subject than attending a formal class.

What a time to catch up on the latest novels! Take the bestseller list, start at the top and read through it. If you reserve books at the library, you'll be notified when they're in and save extra trips with the baby. Involve a few women in a book discussion group. If you rarely find time to read, a discussion group will give you a reason to finish an interesting book.

When you are at home it is important to keep up with what's going on in the world. It's easy to become completely involved in your baby routine and the limited scope of your home. One can quickly fall into lazy intellectual habits. Staying on top of events takes effort. When you catch yourself falling into daily routines that leave you nothing to talk about except babies, it's time to take stock.

Are you reading at least the front page of your newspaper every day?

Do you subscribe to a weekly news magazine? This is important not only for national news, but for news of art, music, theater, sports, and a variety of other subjects.

Do you turn on TV or radio news broadcasts?

Are you keeping up with the literature in your own profession or trade?

Do you subscribe to any special-interest magazines?

YOU: FASCINATING! INTERESTING!

Keep yourself interested and interesting! Banish the phrase,

"I'm just a housewife" from your consciousness.

It's amazing how many opportunities being at home can offer. You are a fascinating, aware person, not one whose mind has turned to play dough from changing diapers and talking baby talk. You have thoughts to express because you read, do, and think. The fact that your husband and friends have jobs doesn't automatically make them more interesting. Think of the parties at which husbands talk only of their work, but somehow it seems all right. They can be just as boring as if you were to talk about babies all evening.

You can be the one who is interesting in a social situation, the one who can spark a dull evening with your new and unique interests and abilities, because you are making a conscious effort to expand your outlook on life. At a party I went to the evening was going from slow to deadly. The hostess, a young mother like myself, changed into a costume and delighted everyone with her Flamenco dancing! If you play the guitar, take it along, and if the evening is slow, pull out the guitar and start everyone singing. Certainly the night will be more memorable than banal cocktail conversations.

Perhaps you are having trouble getting yourself together at home because you are used to the regimentation of a job. Your life at home *is* your job; organize it that way! Make up a to-do list each evening for the next day as you might have done while you were working. Keep it simple. Realize that you can count on only certain time periods to accomplish things. Don't look at your baby as an interference. You must integrate both of your schedules.

You'll be surprised by what you can accomplish during your baby's nap time. If you have a newborn, expect your time to become more regulated around the baby's third or fourth month of life. Your baby will be taking two regular naps a day—usually an hour or so in the morning and two hours or more in the afternoon until about fourteen months old. If you begin to plan that time now, there are at least three hours a day that you have completely to yourself.

Consider what you can create and learn if you put your mind to it. While you're thinking about feeding schedules, think about your own schedule. Maybe you'll want to save the morning nap time to get chores and household paperwork out of the way. Keep the afternoon open for you. For your new interests! For your new self! For the new you!

4

Combating Loneliness

Being at home, working through a daily schedule with your baby can create an unfortunate phenomenon—extreme loneliness.

Who would think a new mother could be lonely? Armed with her precious new baby, a nice apartment or house, perhaps a trusty pet—who could ask for more?

THE NEW MOTHER'S PLIGHT

The truth is, new mothers are among the loneliest people in the world. New babies sleep most of the day, making it difficult to get out. Even when your baby settles into a two-nap-a-day schedule, those non-nap hours are often spent running errands. Days can go by without adult companionship.

Friends without children seem as if they are in another world. You may feel they are insensitive to your baby's schedule and the demands on your time. Not true. They are simply unaware of the time commitment and new responsibility that you have.

You may have thought that neighbors would be a source of friendship. You soon realize that when you are home all day, few other people are.

Even when you attempt to coordinate schedules with friends and their babies, that doesn't always work out. I had tried to get together with my friend Rebecca for months. Jordan was in nursery school three mornings a week. Rebecca and her son Daniel had mother and child classes the alternate mornings. Daniel still took an afternoon nap and Jordan didn't. So we couldn't meet at a mutually convenient time, which added frustration to the loneliness.

Mothers who live in big cities find that many of their close friends live too far away to make a long commute for the sake of adult companionship. By the time they get to where they are going, it's time to turn around and go home because, yes, there are many children who will nap only in their own cribs.

The suburbs, with their large imposing fences, don't make for easy friendships. "Good fences make good neighbors," wrote Robert Frost, but they also make for isolated, lonely mothers. Houses equipped with swing sets, sandboxes and plastic swimming pools are lovely, but to a lonely mother and small child they can seem like little prison playgrounds.

Okay. Sympathy hour is over. It's time to stop feeling sorry for yourself.

FINDING FRIENDS

This is no time to be coy. What you need most of all is a friend with a child of your child's age. March over to the local playground. When you see another mother with a baby in a stroller looking as alone as you feel, break the ice with that age-old phrase: "How old is your baby?" Strike up a conversation. When you find a woman you might like to know better, be friendly and even slightly aggressive. Ask her over for coffee if she lives nearby. Or, perhaps the question, "Would you like to take the kids to McDonalds for lunch?" will meet a happy response. Chances are that she is as lonely as you are. If she's not your type, try again another day. If this woman isn't destined to be your bosom buddy, you have at least talked and interacted with someone that day.

Join a community swimming pool during the summer if you can afford it. It's a natural place to meet new mothers, older mothers, babysitters, *anyone*, because people come on a fairly regular basis. Daily companionship around the pool can help pass many lonely summer hours.

When you're home, you will need several types of friends. You will need friends with whom you can discuss baby problems. You'll need friends who are get-up-and-goers, who do things at the drop of a hat. You will need friends who are interested in a variety of things and can spark your interest in something new. Without this potpourri of friends, you can fall into the habit of spending days with women who do nothing but sit around, drink coffee, and talk about how many times their children had diarrhea that week. I'll never forget one friend who had a baby a few days before I. She launched into descriptive details of the contents of her child's diaper. I asked her if we could please change the subject. We looked at each other with amazement, then laughed at ourselves. Is this what motherhood does to one's brain?

You must get out. Attend a regularly scheduled exercise class during the day, pottery classes, anything that will get you in touch with others in your situation.

Join organizations. You may not plan on being really involved, but you will be able to meet many people by attending meetings and by casually participating in one aspect of the group. Even joining a telephone committee will help you communicate with others every day.

Mother and child classes offered by the YMCA or county

recreation department are another place to acquire friends.

Be a self-starter. Don't be the type of person who always needs companionship to try something new. It's too limiting. You'll never get out. In a new situation, you'll tend to stick with your friend and never meet anyone else.

Motivate yourself to be with and speak to other adults each day. If you don't make a conscious effort to be with people, you can easily let days pass without talking with anyone but your quite unresponsive four-month-old. Husbands who ask, "Talk to anyone today?" often are astonished when a wife answers, "No." Or, "No one but the checker at the supermarket."

Begin to plan your week in advance. Post a calendar with large daily spaces in your kitchen. Make sure there is at least one planned activity scheduled for each week. Mark down events listed in your newspaper that might spark your interest. Call your chamber of commerce and ask for a list of current and future happenings in your city. Note them on your calendar. Invite a friend to attend one of the events.

Join a museum. You'll receive a flyer full of notices for lectures, movies, tours, and a variety of other activities.

Ask a friend over for lunch. It doesn't have to be fancy. Tuna fish is always fine; peanut butter and jelly sandwiches for toddlers. In the summer meet a mom and tot for a picnic.

Assign a library day, an exercise day, a day for exploring someplace new. Those blank spaces will stare at you from the calendar until you fill them. Plan your week so that a day sitting around the house seems like a luxury!

The more you get out, explore, become acquainted with new people and places, the more in touch with yourself you will become—the more you will open your eyes to activities you might want to do by yourself or with your husband for the next few months, or even years!

5

Sexual Crisis? You're Not Alone!

One of the most difficult subjects for new mothers to talk about freely is the resumption of positive sexual relations. The topic is often met with a discouraged look and the comment, "Sex? What's that?" If your vision of going to bed is only a night of sorely needed sleep, you're not alone.

WHAT'S HAPPENING TO YOU?

Resuming positive sexual relations after childbirth is one topic that doctors and childbirth educators rarely discuss. It is not because they are insensitive or trying to keep information from you. They are simply unaware of any problems.

"We don't see many women after their six-week checkup, unless they are being fitted for a diaphragm," a Maryland obstetrician told me. "Most women haven't tried resuming sexual relations at that point."

This was the general consensus of the physicians I questioned about the subject. Most doctors don't realize there is a problem.

Sexual distress after childbirth is common. It is important to recognize the bombardment of physical, hormonal, and emotional changes that are occurring and contributing to a lack of sexual enjoyment.

Many factors are involved. Your body has gone through tremendous physical and hormonal changes. Your sleep patterns are erratic. You are exhausted. Your thoughts are constantly on your new responsibility. You may be attuned only to the cry of your baby, afraid he will wake up the minute you begin your lovemaking.

Perhaps you enjoyed sex in the mornings; now there always seems to be a third person in bed with you at that time, needing to be fed and changed. If you preferred sex at night, you now fall into bed hoping only to sleep as much as you can before the next feeding.

You may be trying new birth control methods. Intercourse itself is often uncomfortable. Penetration can be painful. You may be having trouble with lubrication. You may be experiencing localized pain. Given all of these factors, it is understandable that it may be hard to relax and enjoy yourself.

PRACTICAL SOLUTIONS

Practical solutions can alleviate some of these problems. Difficulty with producing natural lubrication is a phenomenon caused by hormonal changes after childbirth. The problem may occur more often in nursing mothers. The use of a lubricant jelly such as Johnson and Johnson's K-Y Jelly may ease the discomfort. Applying the jelly can become part of your lovemaking.

Pain in a specific area upon penetration may be related to scar tissue resulting from your episiotomy. Experiment and find an intercourse position that will relieve undue pressure on that area. A side-by-side or woman-on-top position may alleviate the pain. It is also helpful if you guide the penis into your body so that you can control the force and degree of penetration.

Your partner's pressure on you to perform after a long absence from sex can be unnerving. Even the most patient and understanding husband might seem like an overeager ogre when you are mentally and physically not ready for sex. If you make a halfhearted effort when you're not anxious for intercourse and you fail, this may stick in your mind the second time around.

APPROACHING PROBLEMS TOGETHER

Communication with your partner is the most crucial element during this time. Don't wait for him to guess what your feelings are. He is not a mind reader. He may also have trouble performing because he is afraid of hurting you. His lack of positive response when you feel confident may be alarming. Together you can work out sexual tensions. Tenderness and understanding are needed between partners and toward each partner at this time.

There are many ways of satisfying each other without intercourse. Try what the noted sex researchers William H. Masters and Virginia Johnson describe as "pleasuring," the process of thinking and feeling sensuously without pressure to proceed with intercourse. Have you ever been turned off by a kiss and a look in your husband's eye, knowing that if you respond, you'll end up having to have intercourse? Develop ways to enjoy each other without thinking of intercourse as the end result. Invest in one of the many paperback books on body massage and follow the suggestions offered. Think of new ways you might turn your husband on, perhaps bringing him to orgasm, or vice versa. Intercourse does not have to be the finale. When you're not concentrating on intercourse, it may happen naturally, pleasurably, without pressure on either partner to perform.

MOTHERS SUGGEST . . .

During several discussion seminars held in gathering material for this book, the subject of resuming sex was raised. Talking out problems in a group was like a consciousness-raising event. A sense of relief prevailed once the discussion was in full swing.

Almost all of the women felt that only they were having difficulties. They assumed everyone else was able to resume blissful relations that were as exciting as before their babies were born. Once the channels of confidence were open, the following situations were exposed as more common than rare and everyone could quickly identify with them.

One woman stated, "When the baby finally went to sleep, I wanted to be totally alone and untouched. I felt like sex was one more assault on my body that I didn't need." At that, the room filled with sounds of mutual agreement.

Several women had considered seeking advice from a marriage counselor. Self-blame was apparent. Few had sized up the total picture. Most tried to deal with the situation as well as they could.

The majority of women did seem to begin to enjoy intercourse again somewhere around three to five months following delivery. Their babies began to sleep through the night and take fairly regular naps. Nursing mothers became less fatigued because there were fewer feedings. They were more comfortable with their role as mothers and their integration of the baby into their lives.

Some related helpful ways they were able to begin their sexual relations anew.

"Make a special date with your husband," suggested one mother. "Mark it on your calendar. That day, prepare for an intimate candlelight dinner. As soon as the baby goes to sleep, dress up as you would to go out for dinner, set the table with good dishes, wine, soft music, the works! The relaxation of the evening, the time put aside only for the two of you, plus the wine, of course, might help to put you in the mood."

Another woman suggested a bubble bath with your mate, accompanied by a bottle of champagne.

Try an X-rated movie! "I had never been to one before," confided JoAnne shyly. "It was my *mother's* idea, would you believe? But, it worked!"

Often, getting the baby out of your immediate proximity can help the situation. Arrange to leave your child with a nearby relative, sitter, or friends for a morning or afternoon. Uninterrupted time for yourselves when you are not exhausted at the end of the day can shed a new light on your hours together.

With each of these suggestions, it is apparent that the women were psychologically ready for intercourse. It was planned. Their minds were on sex throughout each preparation. The woman who suggested having an intimate dinner with her husband was preparing mentally for having positive sexual relations. The same with the bubble bath and the X-rated movie. So much of positive sex for women is mental. When you feel good about yourself, you begin to feel sexy and you can transmit it to whatever you are doing. It happens when you fit into your prepregnancy clothes, again when you buy something new, try a new hairdo, experiment with your makeup, think about yourself and not your baby. As you renew interest in yourself, your needs, the needs of a close relationship with your mate, renewed sexual feelings become important and natural.

Having a child is a stressful and joyful period for both you and your husband. As you conceived and brought your child into the world together, so must you embark on all the new experiences of parenthood together. As your child flourishes, so will your love for each other.

PART II

HOW DO I FIND TIME?

6

Motivation—You Come First

"Find time for yourself? With a baby? Ha!" laughed one new mother. "I wonder if I'll ever have a minute to call my own!" Yet many mothers somehow manage to accomplish activities even when their children are small, because they are forced to make the most efficient use of every scrap of time.

Many women I interviewed felt they were so entrenched in their day-to-day existence that they wouldn't know where to begin to make things easier for themselves.

A mother of an eight-month-old complained that she would "love to take some classes, but I don't have the time. Taking care of the baby, cooking, cleaning, and shopping consume so much of my day that I can never get out."

Another mother was able to accomplish as much while holding down a full-time job.

The key? Motivation and organization.

You may be your own worst enemy when it comes to finding time. Your baby and your home are handy excuses if you want a reason to avoid accomplishing things that are important to you. That goes for quality time with your husband, too, which is certainly something of concern to everyone with the changes a baby brings. It's easy to feel overburdened by your new responsibilities; your world has taken a 360-degree turn. It is also easy to see the proverbial light at the end of the tunnel, just inches away, if you give yourself the chance.

Don't be afraid to erode any excuses. *You come first.* Make a commitment to yourself, not to your housework, not to your grocery shopping, not to your cooking. It's easy to stay home, to take that path of least resistance. Yet how do you feel about yourself when you look in the mirror at the end of the day? At the end of a week? At the end of a month?

You *can* shed those excuses, *can* do what you want for yourself, *can* enjoy tender, meaningful moments with your husband, *can* have quality time with your baby and your family as a whole. When you do, you'll find that being a woman, a mother, a person in today's world is an exciting, expanding, enjoyable experience.

7

Streamlining Housework: You Vs. Acrylic Shine

Which of the following would you like to do today?

Clean bathrooms
Wax floors
Dust
Read a novel
Attend a class in calligraphy
Visit an art museum
Sew a new outfit

Did you answer clean bathrooms? Wax floors? Dust? Probably not. Who would? Are these activities on the top of your list of things to do today? Think about it!

Housework seems to be a top priority on Ann Lansing's list. She sighed as she told me, "I do all of my laundry and shopping in the morning, straighten and clean the house during Brian's afternoon nap time. Then, it's dinner for the baby, bath time and bedtime, while I juggle dinner for us and clean up again. Suddenly, it seems the day is gone. It's nine o'clock. I'm too tired to do anything for myself."

If Ann's routine sounds familiar, it's time to evaluate your priorities.

Let's examine Ann's situation.

She has placed her household chores and everyone else's care first, with time for herself at the end of the day. Her only free time is after nine o'clock. Who feels like starting a project after a full day's demands? She probably has enough energy to turn on the television and doze off— hardly a feeling of self-stimulation for the day. What of her relationship with her husband? What can she look forward to tomorrow? The day after? Only a slight variation on the same theme.

PINPOINT PRIORITIES

Try again, mom! You can change tomorrow! What about *you*? Get up this morning and ask, "What will I do for *me* today?" rather than say, "Today I really must wash the kitchen floor."

Recognize what you want to do for yourself and carve out time from each day to do it. It takes planning, organization, and willpower, but the chores will get done. Once you establish the need for time each day for yourself, you have a reason for organizing and you'll strive to get things done quickly, so nothing erodes your "me" time.

Betty Freidan, in her book, *The Feminine Mystique,* succinctly equates the Peter Principle with housework: "Houseworking tasks always seem to expand to fill all available time. If you have thirty minutes available, they require thirty minutes. If you have eight hours, houseworking tasks magically swell and consume eight hours."

Don't let housework consume all of your time. Learn to run your house; don't let your house run you! Develop a new attitude toward housework. No one really likes a messy house. Be realistic. Are you setting the same standards of perfection for your house that you had before you had a child? How many apple juice spills were on your kitchen floor before you became a mother? How many ground-in cookie crumbs were in your rugs? How many toys did you pick up? How many times did you cook dinner in a day? Many of us strive for utopian standards we established before we had children. No one should expect such perfection now.

ANALYZE YOUR DAY—REORGANIZE

Approach each day in terms of an energy schedule. What part of the day is your most productive time? Early morning? Afternoon? Pinpoint it. Then plan to save that time to accomplish activities that are important to you. Don't waste high-energy productive time on meaningless chores. For example, save housework for low-energy times of the day when your ambition is lagging. If you are tired, and usually kill time by watching TV or with lengthy phone conversations, cut back on the viewing and talking and do easy tasks then. You'll be amazed at how much you'll accomplish!

When the mother of a fourteen-month-old analyzed her routine, she discovered her most unproductive hour was after she had fed the baby dinner and before her husband came home. She said, "Matthew is usually in a playful mood after supper. We make a game out of vacuuming one day, dusting another. Sometimes, I give him a ride on the broom. By the time my husband comes home, we've straightened and cleaned and had fun, too. That unproductive hour of waiting has become fruitful and passes quickly."

"My house is never completely clean all at once," remarked the mother of an eleven-month-old. "I gave up that ideal shortly after the baby came. I straighten one room every day or so. Nothing gets out of hand that way. Or similarly, I vacuum one day, wash floors another, clean bathrooms yet another day. Housework doesn't become all encompassing or exhausting that way. I only do chores when there is absolutely nothing else to do at the time!"

"It's the little jobs that drive me crazy," complained another mother, "so I do them when I'm not so conscious of them—in the early morning. The baby gets up about 6:30 and I give her a bottle. By 7:30 I've usually thrown a load of laundry in the washer, started breakfast, made a sandwich for my husband, and mixed formula for the day. We're both home then, so one of us can keep an eye on Jill. By 8:15 everyone is fed, the beds are made and the dishes are in the dishwasher. Jill takes her morning nap around 8:30. Then I shower leisurely and wake up. It seems most of those repetitive daily tasks were accomplished when I was half asleep!"

"That's fine when you have a small baby," smirked the mother of an eighteen-month-old, "but once your child starts crawling, pulling up, and walking you can forget that schedule! Flexibility is the key. When David was an infant and on a two-nap-a-day schedule, he'd awaken early and we'd play with him until John went to work. During his nap at 8:30, I'd do the dishes, beds, etc., take a shower and dress. When he gave up his morning nap, I was almost ready to give up. If I tried to put the dishes in the dishwasher, David would crawl up and reach for the knives, or pull out a plate. It was impossible. I didn't know what to do with him while I showered; he'd always get into something. So, I changed my schedule. The breakfast dishes had to wait until lunchtime to be washed. I showered at night or in the early morning while my husband was still home."

Another woman in a discussion group concurred, but she rearranged her schedule differently. "I hated to spend nap time cleaning, but when Carolyn started crawling and toddling, I had little choice. I accomplished twice as much in half the time when she wasn't around. So I set aside only two of her afternoon naps each week for cleaning. As she grew older and learned to play by herself, I found I could do more of the chores during her waking hours and use more nap time hours for hobbies I enjoyed. I began to needlepoint. Now I design my own canvases, which I am beginning to sell through a local needlework shop."

Everyone agreed that to a nonmother, simple activities such as showering, cleaning dishes, and making beds do not appear to be much of a problem. But to a mother with a small baby, each tiny aspect of her daily life becomes an obstacle to conquer. Once she seems to have everything perfectly coordinated, and a routine settled, the child moves into another stage and the balloon bursts. Rethinking, replanning, and the need to be flexible go into effect. An infant is somewhat oblivious to the sound of a vacuum cleaner. An eight-month-old may be petrified by it. By the age of twenty months, the child sees the vacuum cleaner as the most exciting object in the world and insists on having a turn.

"Things do get better!" claim the mothers of three-year-olds!

HELP! HUSBANDS AND HOUSEKEEPERS

Husbands generally are a major help to many women. Here are some of the comments taped during several interviews held around the country. Similar situations occurred from coast to coast differing only slightly among the individuals involved.

"After I got over the shock of the alterations in my life," related a woman in Florida, "I sat down with my husband and said, 'Look, I really need some help.' He was a doll about the whole thing. While he was always helpful with chores before, he became unstoppable. Sometimes he made *me* feel guilty. He would walk in the house, kiss me hello, take out the garbage and straighten up. It was a great relief for me at the end of the day. I was able to make dinner without dozens of interruptions; I could even relax for ten minutes. The extra time we chiseled out of the day for ourselves later in the evening was delightful."

"Talking to my husband about his expectations of me was a revelation!" exclaimed a Boston woman. "Some things I did for him before we had the baby were really not so important. I thought it was important to *him* that the house be hospital clean all the time, but he didn't really care. I discovered I was my own worst enemy on that score. He also made me aware that it was I who insisted on fancy meals every night; he said he could be happy with leftovers, tuna fish, and eggs. Once I overcame some of my own hang-ups about being a superwife, life became easier. Our house is clean and I make gourmet meals sometimes, because I like to cook. But neither is as important in the total scheme of my time. I'm not frantic or compulsive about them. We have more time for us."

In my own situation, my husband has always been a willing help. But the house still seemed a disaster. We discussed the problem. We determined that our most unproductive time was Sunday night after an early dinner. Now we both pitch in and clean the apartment from top to bottom, taking turns watching Jordan and including him in some of the chores. He enjoys watching all of the movement. With the two of us tackling the work as a team, we clean the entire apartment in about an hour and a half. We do a thorough job twice a month, alternating chores as required. I vacuum, wash floors and dust as is needed between major clean-ups.

Try this idea offered by a San Diego couple.

"We keep a chore board on the refrigerator. We make a to-do list at the beginning of the week. Whenever one of us does a chore, it's crossed off. Everything is accomplished without nagging, though sometimes we strike bargains which makes some fun out of it, too. We both know we have responsibilities and we take care of them."

One Baltimore couple, both physicians in training, have two children, ages twenty months and three months. They have very little time. "We do housework with the children in tow. Jim backpacks the older boy while he vacuums, while I do dishes and dust with the baby in a chest carrier."

There are many husbands, however, who would rather trek across Outer Mongolia than change a diaper or push a vacuum cleaner. If your husband falls into this category, changing his feelings may take time. It may never happen. Do discuss his attitudes with him. Outline some of the chores that you find unnerving and difficult to do with the baby. Ask him which would be easier for him to do. He may surprise you and be happy to do many things for himself that you previously volunteered to do, such as drop off clothing at the cleaner, pick up parcels at the post office, or sort and pair his own socks.

When your spouse does agree to assume some tasks, don't expect him to do them the way you do. Said one young woman, "I hate the way my husband makes the bed, but I'm thankful he does it and I compliment him." Another admitted, "My husband's Navy experience with kitchen duty shined through when I asked him to help; I learned several short cuts from him!"

Of course, a major relief for the problems of housework is to hire housekeeping help if your budget permits it. If you can afford cleaning help only occasionally, use it for major chores, not for the everyday dishwashing, bed making, juice spills, and toy clean-up. Plan to use help efficiently to ease your heavy work loads. Many women feel that other people will not do as good a job as they would like. But, if you can afford it, and cleaning helps free you to do more important things, then hire help at least twice a month. Think how good you will feel if you know you have that time to yourself for a game of tennis, a trip to an art gallery, or a picnic with the baby at a new park. You'll soon treasure your newfound hours.

Organizing your housework is a matter of priorities. Once you establish that *you* are more important than the acrylic shine on your floor, you're on the road to more rewarding and stimulating days ahead.

8

Simplifying Your Cooking and Shopping

Eating three meals a day is a pleasurable part of life. Preparing them, however, can be a different matter. Whether the meals you serve consist of chateaubriand or hamburger helper, they take time. They must be planned. Food has to be purchased and prepared, followed by the inevitable clean-up. Now a new character enters this routine scene: your baby! That whirling dervish who can pull cans off the grocer's shelf faster than a speeding bullet, scream louder than the whir of your mixmaster, and pluck glasses from your dishwasher with the skill of a magician. This little cherub also needs a specially prepared menu that changes at various stages of his development.

How to cope?

Call the paper and place an ad for a cook? Sounds good but a bit dramatic. More practical are ideas from some of us who have met the challenge of mealtimes. We have learned to get out of the kitchen quickly and move on to more exciting things!

"Before Michael was born," recalled the mother of a two-year-old, "I usually started preparing dinner an hour before we planned on eating. As if on cue, Michael's cranky time always began around five o'clock. Making dinner at that time was a joke! Then I discovered the electric slow cooker appliance. I could prepare complete meals such as pot roasts, chicken, soups, and stews in the early morning while Michael napped, and forget about them until we were ready to sit down for dinner. All I had to do was toss a salad or fix a vegetable. I considered that appliance a live-in cook!"

COOKING FOR YOUR BABY

I haven't yet talked to a mother who hasn't gone through a five o'clock fussy period with a child, often referred to as "the arsenic hour." It's a time when your child is hollering while you're trying to prepare his dinner, feed him, clean up, and start dinner for you and your husband. This pleasure comes at the end of your day when all you feel like doing is putting up your feet, sipping a glass of wine, and listening to some music. Oh, well!

Organizing your baby's food is a first step in lessening the horror of the arsenic hour. When your child's food can be served quickly and without lengthy preparation, part of the battle is won. Your baby requires a balanced meal three times a day, seven days a week. When you think about it (perhaps it's better if you don't!), it is a formidable, infinite task. Your goal is to make food preparation as easy and efficient as you can.

We've been programmed to believe that buying prepared baby foods is the easiest and fastest way to go. Today, however, an alternative is to prepare the baby's food yourself. Before you cringe at the thought, hear the arguments. Making your own baby food is definitely more economical, unquestionably more nutritious, and surprisingly simple. And if you organize your baby food, making it might take a maximum of twenty minutes a week.

How can making food be easier than opening a jar? Consider the time you spend selecting special baby foods at the store, lugging the bottles home, and putting them away. And how about those emergency trips when you run out? Now, open your refrigerator. There are probably three or four foods that you could easily turn into baby food while you're making tonight's supper. Here's how.

Are you cooking a roast this evening? Baked chicken? Meat loaf? Cook the following vegetables along with your meal and you'll have vegetables for two weeks.

Carrots

Wrap scraped carrots in aluminum foil with a little water. Put them in the oven while the chicken is baking. After twenty minutes, the carrots will be soft. Put the carrots in a blender, food processor, or baby food grinder, add a little water or apple juice, and puree.

Squash

Bake acorn or banana squash along with chicken or a roast. Place squash skin side up in a glass dish with enough water to cover the bottom. Squash will be cooked after fifty minutes. Scrape from rind and puree with a little water or juice.

Sweet Potatoes or Yams

Bake one hour or more, depending on size and temperature of your oven. Scrape from skins, mash with a fork, and puree.

For storage, use the frozen food cube method. Fill each section of an empty ice cube tray with carrots or yams. Cover with foil and freeze. When you want to serve your baby carrots, pop out a carrot cube, defrost, and warm up.

Chicken, meats, fish, various fruits, and green vegetables can be cooked, pureed, and stored in frozen cubes.

Freeze different food cubes and combine a whole meal in a plastic bag. Run the bag under hot water to defrost, then heat and serve. If you own a microwave oven, this process will take only a few minutes.

With homemade food you'll always have ample supplies in a wide variety. I learned how easy it was to put a whole chicken in the slow cooker. The meat would fall off the bones, and I could make up an entire tray of chicken cubes. Pears, peaches, and apples can be put into the slow cooker or oven to poach until you have time for them. A microwave oven can do all of this in a matter of minutes.

Look for family foods that can be adapted to baby. Mott's, Seneca, and many supermarket house brands make an unsweetened natural applesauce with only apples and water. Bananas are the easiest to prepare; just mash with a fork. There's little need to buy jarred bananas that are laced with fattening tapioca. Remember, it doesn't matter to the baby whether you serve the same meal three days in a row. Do what is easiest for you.

Being able to regulate the consistency of food as your child grows is another advantage of making your own baby food. It's easier to introduce your baby gradually to table food when he or she is used to the taste of these foods, rather than food that has been sweetened, salted, and watered down.

Organize formula making, too. Many mothers mix formula early each morning when the baby is screaming for it; both mother and baby become frenetic. You may find it wiser to mix formula immediately after dinner while you are still in the kitchen or to prepare formula before going to bed to eliminate the morning madness. If you have a microwave oven, you can heat a bottle in about thirty seconds.

COPING WITH THE MESS

Cooking baby food has an inevitable follow-up: it must be fed to a baby who has a natural tendency to grab the spoon from your hand and fling food everywhere. When your baby wants to handle the food, decorating the walls and floors with splattered baby food becomes a great pastime. Add this clean-up time for the baby, the surrounding area, and you to your schedule! One mother made a vinyl kimono for herself to use during this interior-decorating stage. Variations are available in kitchen accessory stores; they help considerably to avoid globs of rice cereal randomly appliqued on your clothes.

As your child develops and grows to high-chair age, nothing will be more disgusting than your walls and floor. To simplify clean-up, spread newspapers under the high chair at feeding time, then gather them and throw them out when you're through. If that's unesthetic, plastic floor pads used under office rolling chairs are available from office supply and furniture stores; they wipe clean easily, are neat looking, and will reduce floor cleaning. Any large piece of heavy plastic will do. For walls, if you don't have vinyl wallpaper or wipe-clean Contact paper behind the baby's chair, fashion a piece of bright vinyl with two grommets at the top, put two nails in the wall, and hang it up. Depending on your kitchen and the type of vinyl you select, it will look like a bright graphic behind the baby's chair, and it's removable and washable.

FAMILY MEALTIME EFFICIENCY

Now that you have your baby fed and freshened, how about dinner for you and the rest of the family? Not as easy as it used to be, is it? With a little organization, and some ideas from the following mothers, you'll free yourself from that position over the hot stove fast.

"I used to be a stickler for serving elegant meals," mentioned one mother. "Every night I prepared some form of meat, a vegetable, and a tossed salad. I'd try at least one new foreign dish every week. After the baby was born the effort of hunting up recipes and shopping for unusual ingredients became an aggravation and frustration instead of an adventure in cooking. Now, I rely on casseroles and meals that I can put in my slow cooker. I try to make enough for a few dinners at a time and freeze the extras. Instead of an involved salad, I may slice a tomato. I save making new and exotic dishes for nights when my husband and I have time to cook together and eat leisurely, or for company. I've changed my thinking: meals are necessities, not gourmet delights each evening. We've both slimmed down as well!"

Lynn, the mother of two toddlers, said she "never really liked leftovers, but now, I always plan for them. I try to prepare enough food so that I can serve it alternate days later in another form. That way, we don't eat the same thing two days in a row. There's usually something to feed the children when we go out."

Cook meals in bulk to make life easier. Freeze meals such as spaghetti sauce, lasagna, or stews in serving portions. Having something in the freezer to fall back on when you're too tired to cook or haven't had a chance to get to the store can be a lifesaver.

Some women find that it's efficient to prepare dinner and partially cook meals after lunch while they are still in the kitchen. At dinner time, they pop the dish into the oven for that final few-minute warm-up.

FUNDAMENTALS OF GROCERY SHOPPING

Many mothers voiced the opinion that meals often aren't the main difficulty. It's getting to the grocery store that is their biggest problem.

"Once I have food in the refrigerator, I can usually come up with something!"

Grocery shopping can be a horror story. Mothers describe situations in which their children have climbed out of the grocer's cart while their backs were turned, pulled down stacks of cereal, eaten fruit from the display, and screamed throughout the whole process.

When your baby is very young, you may be able to shop

with her easily. Lay the baby in an infant seat at the top of the grocery cart, or carry her in a chest carrier. An infant is often delighted with the changing colors of displays and the fluorescent lights. At about four months of age the picture changes. Your baby will become more active, and she may flip the carrier over. The next step is to wedge the baby in the front of the cart in an upright position, using towels, receiving blankets, or coats. One mother goes straight to the paper towel section, takes down two packages, and puts one on either side of the baby. Before checkout she puts them back.

Children are usually little trouble to take to the store until they are old enough to climb out of the basket, or vocal enough to scream "Out!" when you've only gotten to the fruits and vegetables.

"Jodi was fine to take to the store for a while," lamented the mother of a twenty-one-month-old. "Then she became impossible. Absolutely hated it. I'd stuff her with crackers, cookies, anything, but it became such an effort that it was easier to go without her. I found going alone to the store in the early evening while my husband watched Jodi was much simpler. There are usually fewer people in the store and shorter checkout lines then. I can get in and out more quickly and efficiently, and my husband helps me unload the car."

Another solution. "There's nothing I hate more than grocery shopping with Aaron. It's especially difficult in the winter with coats on and off, getting him in and out of the car seat, and lugging the groceries into the house and putting them away. I do a heavy shopping trip twice a month and shop mostly for meats, canned and frozen goods. Each night before my husband comes home, he calls and asks me what I need. He will pick up fresh fruits, vegetables, milk, juice, and bread as needed. It's easier for him to make short stops more frequently than for me to go through that whole ordeal."

A word of caution: If your husband does the shopping, don't criticize his purchases. One woman reports, "My husband inevitably buys economy packs of a product and claims he's saving money, though we may not use it up in ten years. If I ask him to pick up three of something and they are six for a dollar, he'll buy the six. No harm is done, really, and it saves wear and tear on me."

A system that may work for you is to make out a menu for the entire month. Many women's magazines and newspaper food sections have suggested menus. Check off the meals you want to make. Organize your shopping list so you know exactly what you need and can plan accordingly.

A list is imperative. If you forget anything, which is easy to do if the baby is fussing, that means either another trip to the store (a fate worse than death), or doing without. "I've altered enough recipes with substitute ingredients to write an entire cookbook!" laughed one mother.

When staples are on sale, such as toilet tissue, paper towels, or soap, buy them in quantity; one less thing to forget next week.

Planning, shopping, cooking, and cleaning up after meals are a large part of daily existence that you can't avoid. These activities need not consume an inordinate portion of your day. Aprons away, mom! We've got more exciting things to do!

PART III

WHAT DO I WANT TO DO?

9

Setting Goals: Short Term/Long Term

Women are searching. Each is trying to find her individual niche in life, something she likes to do and can do well. Something that she can take pride in calling her profession.

Some women are fortunate. They know what they like to do and are able to practice their professions with pleasure. Other women relate that they disliked previous jobs, perhaps were unhappy with the career choices made in their college days. They were delighted to be home, not doing what they disliked. But the same women admitted they wanted to find something they could do and do well.

Many women I interviewed appeared to be waiting for divine inspiration to hit them over the head one day with what they want to do for the next months, years, or a lifetime. Few thought little about actively taking time to analyze their own needs, to ask, "What is it I really want to do? What do I like to do?" and find definite answers. Whatever it is, it must be something that satisfies you, not society's view of what you should be doing.

A friend of mine has been going through these thought processes for years. She has always taken a circuitous route, selecting from a variety of professions that make her sound good, for which she could seek approval. Perhaps her parents would pat her on the head and say, "my daughter the computer expert," or "my daughter the nurse." I used to cringe every time she talked about a new career. She stayed at each job for a few months at most and then would fill the time in between jobs by selling records or cosmetics until another bright career idea lit up her enthusiasm.

There is nothing wrong with picking careers as you would pick a bouquet for your table. You never know when new ideas will spark your imagination and give you insight into new goals. But careful examination of your needs can lead to a more satisfying path than the one my friend continues to take.

First of all, forget society. You'll never be a success or enjoy yourself if you're trying to please someone else. Your goals do not have to be career oriented as defined by a college career counselor. Choose something that might be fun. If you don't like what you're doing, you'll never do it well.

For fun, and to get out of the house one evening a week, Laura Manning enrolled in a calligraphy class. Laura enjoyed the class, practiced in her spare hours, and in time became an excellent calligrapher. She now teaches calligraphy through the adult education department of her local university.

Anna Goldstein had been enthusiastic about photography before her child was born. She had taken one or two courses but never as many as she had wanted. After Joshie's birth, Anna took some smashing candid shots of her new baby. She read up on camera techniques and shot innumerable rolls of film on sunny days and overcast days, taking notes on lighting and exposures. Romps in the park took on a new meaning. The zoo was a heaven. She took pictures of neighbors' children. Everyone was impressed with her insights and poses of children and much preferred her photos to studio portraits. Word got out, and soon Anna was able to establish herself as a freelance children's photographer.

Gretchen Rhinelander likes to cook. She enjoys entertaining. She teaches an adult education course once a week on "The Ease of Entertaining." She also teaches a cake-decorating class one afternoon a week in her home during daughter Kelly's nap. Once a month Gretchen gives food processor demonstrations at a local gourmet shop.

None of these women would have thought a few years ago that their fun could be channeled into new careers. Before her baby was born, Laura taught kindergarten; Anna was a lab technician and Gretchen an executive secretary. Each charted a new course for her life by doing something that really appealed to her.

Who knows where all these new activities might lead? Laura talks about setting up a business doing calligraphy for invitations, menus, stationery—a variety of work. Anna may develop her own photography studio, employing photographers to work for her. Gretchen has considered starting a catering business. Each may expand on something she loves doing more than her previous career. Being at home gave them time to discover new potentials.

I'm not only discussing careers here, but examples of how you can improve your life on a day-to-day basis as well; perhaps leading to a goal, perhaps only providing enjoyment for the moment. The main objective is to focus on a more stimulated, happier you. A you whose days are filled doing what you enjoy as a person, a mother, a woman.

GOAL-SETTING EXERCISES

Let's explore what you like to do and plan an attack for your new improved life!

Right now, take out several pieces of paper, a pen or pencil, and a timer. You are about to do some exercises to find out more about yourself and your goals, to begin planning for more stimulating days ahead. Before you start, be sure you have at least half an hour of uninterrupted time.

First page:

Take three minutes. Write down all the things you like to do, such as reading, skiing, painting, traveling, and so on.

Second page:

Take three minutes. Write down everything you would like to do in your life. Jot down anything that comes to mind, no matter how bizarre or kinky. You're the only one who is going to read this.

Third page:

Take three minutes. Write down what you would like to be doing in the next three to five years.

Next, spread out the three sheets. Look for similarities in each sheet. Circle the answers that recur.

On a fourth sheet, write down the answers you have circled.

On this fourth sheet, staring you right in the face, are things you like to do, things you would like to do eventually, things that you feel are important to your happiness. How can you begin to incorporate these things into your life?

KAREN: ONE MOTHER'S GOAL SHAPING

Here's an actual case history of twenty-seven-year-old Karen, mother of three-month-old Elyse. She is a high school teacher by profession but hasn't worked in over a year. She moved from Philadelphia to Albuquerque soon after she became pregnant and hadn't looked for a job in her new city. Karen had enjoyed teaching English, but hoped for some way to advance her career at a future time, perhaps attaining a degree in counseling.

Karen worked through the goal-setting exercises you've just done. Let's review her answers and consider some of the ways she might begin to attain her goals on a day-to-day basis.

Things I Like to Do

Travel with David
Read
Play with the baby
Ski
Hike
Garden
Walk in the woods
Try new foods
Travel
Explore
Attend interesting lectures
Meet new people
Look good
Exercise
Be with friends
Decorate the house
Read historical novels
Teach
Write poetry
Go to museums and galleries
Collect prints
Hunt for antiques

What I Would Like to Do with My Life

Travel with David
Collect art or antiques in one field, be knowledgeable about it
Some aspect of teaching, perhaps advance in my field
Publish a book of poems
Look great, dress well
Live in a beautiful home
Grow and discover with David
Achieve status in the community
Raise responsible, happy children

What I'd Like to Do in the Next Three to Five Years

Travel with David
Discover and explore New Mexico
Perhaps have another child
Begin to collect art and artifacts for the house
Write poetry
Become an active part of the community by serving on various committees
Decorate the house
Take a course in something new
Begin graduate school in counseling
Discover my own sense of style, look good, feel sharp in my dress

Here is the list gleaned from her answers to our four questions:

1. Travel, explore with husband.
2. Look and dress well.
3. Achieve status in the community.
4. Collect art, become knowledgeable about one area.
5. Slowly decorate the house.
6. Advance in the teaching field.
7. Write poetry.

Now, we asked Karen to put her choices in order of descending importance to her at this time, regardless of obstacles. We told her not to worry about baby-sitters, etc., or to think of reasons she couldn't do it, just list priorities.

Her first priority is to travel and explore with her husband. How can she strive for that goal during the next week?

1. She can arrange an afternoon excursion with her husband and hire a sitter to watch the baby: perhaps lunch, then a gallery or a museum tour.

2. She can plan a day trip, take the baby in a chest carrier, explore the countryside, have a picnic.

Her second priority at this time is to look and dress well. (Don't we all feel that after having a baby?)

1. Karen might pick up a magazine that focuses on new styles for the season and examine how the models wear their hair, makeup, and so on. (You can get so far out of touch during pregnancy.)

2. She could also call the local YMCA, YWCA, or a community center, and ask about dance/exercise classes.

Her third priority is gradually to decorate their new but empty home. While she is thumbing through magazines that offer new styles, she can also delve into decorating magazines to get ideas for her home and start developing a sense of style.

A fourth priority is to achieve some status in her new community. Karen could call the membership chairman of an organization that interests her and ask to be invited to a new members' tea, or inquire about their next regular meeting.

Her fifth priority is to begin collecting art. She could start by checking out an art history or art collecting book from the local library.

Karen's sixth priority is to write poetry. While she's at the grocery store, she can pick up a spiral notebook and begin to jot down thoughts for poems.

Her final priority is to advance in the teaching field. She can call the local university and inquire about a graduate degree program.

Observe that none of the achievements here is monumental. But each is a positive step toward Karen's achievement of things she'd like to do.

The schedule for Karen's upcoming week might look like this:

1. Pin down a time her husband can take a vacation. Begin to discuss where they might like to go.
2. Make an appointment to have her hair done. Take an exploratory shopping trip to a mall and get an idea of what styles she likes—a good place for a stroller ride!
3. Call the decorating service of a local department store. Make an appointment with the decorator to come to Karen's house to take measurements and offer suggestions.
4. Attend a meeting of the organization that interests her.
5. Browse through the art history book.
6. Read the information received on graduate degree program.
7. Begin to write thoughts and feelings in her journal.

The third week, Karen advances toward her goals through the following actions.

1. She calls a travel agent and asks for literature on vacation spots.
2. She has her hair cut and styled and attends an exercise class.
3. She meets with the decorator for ideas.

4. She signs up for a committee within the organization she chose.
5. She contacts the local museum and inquires about lectures, tours, classes.
6. She makes an appointment to see a counselor at the university regarding returning to school.
7. She continues to write in her journal.

During the fourth week Karen might take the following steps.

1. Discuss travel literature with husband, finances and possibility of vacation, perhaps plan another day trip.
2. Spend an afternoon shopping.
3. Discuss decorating ideas with husband.
4. Hold a committee meeting at her home.
5. Attend an art lecture.
6. Meet with the university counselor.
7. Continue to write in her journal; perhaps check out some poetry books from the library.

Review all the steps for Karen's first month of personal advancement. What do you notice? No major development is evident, yet every weekly step places Karen closer to the goals she wants to attain now and in the future. She is satisfying immediate needs while she builds for later goals. Each week she accomplishes more. Let's go back and see how easy her goal-shaping weeks have been.

Activities Done at Home	**Trips Outside**
Week One	
1. Call YMCA, etc.	1. Day trip with husband.
2. Call organization.	2. Trip to library.
3. Call university.	3. Magazines and journal (done while at grocery store).

Activities Done at Home	**Trips Outside**
Week Two	
1. Discuss vacation plans with husband.	1. Possible exploratory shopping trip.
2. Call for hair appointment.	2. Exercise class.
3. Call decorating service.	3. Attend meeting.
4. Read art history book.	
5. Read through university information.	
6. Begin to make entries in journal.	
Week Three	
1. Call travel agent.	1. Have hair done.
2. Meet at home with decorator.	2. Sign up for committee.
3. Call local museum.	3. Exercise class.
4. Make appointment to see counselor.	
5. Write in journal.	
Week Four	
1. Discuss travel information with husband.	1. Afternoon shopping.
2. Discuss decorating ideas with husband.	2. Attend art lecture.
3. Hold committee meeting at home.	3. See the counselor.
	4. Exercise class.
	5. Pick up poetry books at library while returning art history book.

Karen has accomplished quite a bit in her month of goal shaping! She enjoyed a day trip with her husband. She gathered information about a possible vacation and began to plan for it. She explored the latest fashions and feels chic in her new hairstyle. She shopped. She began attending an exercise class. She collected several new decorating ideas. Karen met people in the community at the organization she joined. She explored new areas of art and attended a lecture. She took initial steps toward a degree in counseling. She began a poetry journal.

What about the baby? What does Karen do with Elyse on her trips out?

Elyse went along with Karen and David on their first day trip to the country. Next time, Karen plans to hire a woman to care for Elyse while she and David visit galleries and have lunch.

On visits to the library, trips to the grocery store to look at magazines, and the exploratory shopping trip at the mall, Elyse went along in a chest carrier or stroller.

While Karen exercised, Elyse gurgled with glee from her infant seat as she watched her mom and others jump, twirl, and bend—a marvelous mobile! During the last exercise, Elyse fussed. Karen held her in her arms while she did the leg part of the exercise. The class does have sitter services available for Elyse when she becomes too active for the infant seat.

Karen joined an organization whose membership consists of many young mothers. A baby sitter is available at each meeting.

A friend offered to watch Elyse while Karen went to the beauty shop and also when she met with the college counselor. Karen has considered joining a baby-sitting cooperative, anticipating future child care needs.

David baby-sat for Elyse while Karen shopped on a Saturday, and for a few hours during the evening of the art lecture. For the next lecture they will go together and hire a sitter.

Karen was able to accomplish a lot for herself with her baby along and had competent sitters to take care of Elyse when she needed them. In no way was Elyse an obstacle to Karen's achievements.

As Elyse grows older, Karen will need to adapt to changes in Elyse's development. She can take advantage of sitter services, play groups, the baby-sitting co-op, a variety of options that will be advantageous for Karen and aid in Elyse's social development with other children. And as Elyse grows, mothering will become more rewarding, and Karen will want to make special time for sharing the precious moments of childhood with her daughter.

Convinced? When you appreciate how one mother organized her life, you can zero in on yours!

On your fourth piece of paper, follow the steps Karen took. List the subjects in descending order of importance to you. Think about how you can begin to reach your number one priority in some small way this week. Next, your number two priority, and so forth.

Now, see how many of the activities can be done while you are at home, how many trips outside the house. Begin to plan your day, your week. Use your phone as much as possible to obtain information.

Each week becomes a step in the stairway to attaining your goals.

You *can* take charge of your life. What an exhilarating feeling when you are in control!

Who says motherhood is a bore? What a terrific time of your life!

10

In a Dilemma? Women's Resource/Counseling Centers

You've worked through the goal-setting exercises. You have a vague idea of possible goals. You don't know how to begin to carry them out. You need more direction, input from someone more knowledgeable, more resourceful. You need more exposure to outside influences—a group, a lecture series, a workshop that can guide you along a more secure path. You may be aware of your goals, but you don't have the resources to put you in touch with the proper people or places. A woman's resource/counseling center may be your answer.

What is a woman's resource center?

It is a center created specifically to deal with answers to the problems women face today. Centers stress such topics as career choices, goal identification, assertiveness training, multiple roles, stress management, financial management, legal problems, and other subjects pertinent to women in today's society. Women's centers are staffed by professionals. They offer workshops, seminars, lectures, and personal counseling.

Some centers are sponsored by county or state agencies, some by colleges and universities. Others are run by the YWCA. Many private agencies also offer counseling services and workshops. Some resource centers are free; others are non-profit organizations that charge nominal fees or fees determined by your income. There are private centers that assess hefty amounts for their services. I'd like to describe a few centers to give you an idea of what they offer, and end with a list of how and where to find centers in your area.

COUNTY AND STATE CENTERS

New Phase and its sister organization, A Woman's Place, in Rockville, Maryland, are sponsored by the Montgomery County Commission for Women. New Phase bills itself as a Career Readiness Center for Women. New Phase offers a series of five regular workshops as well as individual counseling. All services are offered completely free of charge.

Workshops are offered in sequence. Workshop I is an hour-and-a-half session on skills assessment. It is designed to put you in touch with your strongest assets. Workshop II focuses on goal identification. This is similar to the exercises we went through previously. Workshop III is on resume writing. Workshop IV zeros in on job hunt strategies. Workshop V deals with interview techniques. In addition, New Phase sponsors special workshops and group discussion on careers in sales, career aspirations, stress management, and multiple roles (woman, wife, mother, career person). After attending the five basic workshops, you meet with a counselor and begin to explore your options.

A Woman's Place describes itself as a resource and activity center for women, organized to help women make choices about lifestyles and life's work. A Woman's Place offers ongoing activities and resources on a scheduled basis, including employment counseling, referrals for professional services, information about college courses designed around women's needs, recreational programs, education for family development, and group discussions on shared needs, concerns, and solutions. Ongoing sessions are also scheduled concerning women's awareness, separation and divorce, assertive behavior training, sexuality and selfhood, and others. Special courses focus on topics such as women and work, women and the law. Seminars are also offered on women's health, child care, male-female communications, and other topics of interest. A Woman's Place also holds a biweekly drop-in coffee and conversation. Most services are provided free of charge.

UNIVERSITY WOMEN'S CENTERS

Universities offer a wide range of counseling services. State schools usually provide these services free of charge; private colleges often charge a fee. Note that these services are not only for women considering returning to school. They offer self-exploratory counseling to consider all options in your life.

The Women's Center at the University of California, Santa Barbara, offers a wide range of pertinent programs. Within their Women's Re-entry Program, they offer a support group, a workshop on career and life planning for women in transition, a time management workshop, and a learning readiness workshop for re-entry women under the heading of Careers and Employment. There are a forum on women in science careers; workshops called Working with Your Hands, Flexible, Nontraditional Careers for Women, New Ways to Work: Search for Flexibility, and Job Resources for Women in Santa Barbara County; a discussion on breaking out of the clerical track; and an interviewing workshop. There are consciousness-raising groups, assertiveness training workshops, a mothers and children group, mothers' support groups, workshops for those with math anxiety, and a discussion group on women and anger. Special events include a graduate women's potluck dinner, a women and running workshop, a backpacking trip for women, and a symposium on women's health issues.

Other services of the Women's Center include a bulletin

board with information regarding careers, employment opportunities, the ERA, politics, housing, women in transition, announcements, and upcoming programs. Child care is provided at selected meetings. Counseling for re-entry women concerning careers, re-entry to UCSB, and other life changes is available by appointment. The Women's Center resource room contains information and materials on women's issues and concerns, including books, newsletters, topic files, periodicals, research papers, career information, women's studies bulletins, and information on local, state, and national women's organizations. The resource room materials are available to everyone. The room is staffed by the CETA Woman's Resource Project. The speakers' source files contain a comprehensive listing of women prominent in their fields of expertise.

For further information on university counseling services, refer to the women's counseling section in chapter 12.

PRIVATE NONPROFIT/PROFIT WOMEN'S CENTERS

Private counseling centers vary widely in what they offer and the fees they charge. Some are nonprofit organizations. One such center is Applied Potential, a counseling service for women in Highland Park, Illinois.

Applied Potential offers personal, occupational, and educational counseling. It is directed by professional counselors. Applied Potential's purpose is to provide an opportunity for women to analyze their experience, talents, and aspirations. Through individual counseling, group discussions, or one-day seminars, women study questions like these:

> What special talent or interest should I develop?
> Should I return to school?
> Why is my present occupation not satisfying, and what changes can I make?
> How can I learn to be more assertive?

Other services include an information bank with extensive

files on occupations and career-related study programs, an education directory, and a women's guide to education in the Chicago area. Applied Potential also has extensive files on returning to school and professional volunteer jobs.

An initial interview is arranged to decide which services are appropriate for you. A fee is charged for services.

Some resource centers may be slick and expensive operations, although run by very qualified and successful counselors. While these counseling centers serve a purpose for some, my advice would be to seek out free services or those from nonprofit organizations first.

WHERE IS A CENTER IN YOUR CITY?

How do you find out about resource/counseling centers in your area? Try the following:

1. Thumb through the white pages of your phone book. Large cities will probably have listings under the headings of Women or Commission on the Status of Women. I found no such listing in the Albuquerque phone book, so I called the City of Albuquerque information number and was directed to the Commission on the Status of Women in New Mexico. I was transferred to its public information officer, who listed all the places to find women's resource centers in the area.
2. Call your local university and inquire about a woman's center. Also call the counseling center and ask about counselors who are sympathetic to older women returning to school or making career changes.
3. Check with your local library. Not only will you find pamphlets about women's centers, but libraries often have a copy of a city's directory of community resources for your area.
4. Call your local YWCA. Many run seminars on some of the topics discussed earlier.
5. Call your local church or synagogue. Many offer family counseling.

6. Write to Catalyst, a national nonprofit organization that provides career information and self-guidance materials for women. Ask for their publication, *National Network of Local Resource Centers.* Their bibliographies list and case history profiles list are also of interest. Write for these, along with their brochure: Catalyst, 14 East 60th St., New York, NY 10022.

7. If you live in a rural area, contact your county extension office. It often is aware of services for women in a wide range of rural areas.

When you do see a counselor, remember that a counselor will not give you specific answers to your problems. A counselor will help you explore various options available to you. Individual counseling may be the initial contact at a center. Then, the counselor may suggest that you attend various workshops. Or you may be required to take a battery of workshops to make you aware of a wide variety of options, then meet with a counselor after you have a clear view of your abilities and possible goals.

Women's resource/counseling centers are there to help. Don't feel intimidated. They are staffed by highly skilled, caring professionals who are trained to help you explore your fullest potential. They are women working for women. Try one; the experience may change your life.

PART IV
WHAT ARE MY OPTIONS?

11

Volunteerism: A Doorway to Your Future

With your goal-shaping list in hand, let's explore your options and how they can work for you. For a new mother with fragmented time, volunteerism can be the first step over the threshold to a fascinating future.

What is volunteerism?

Bake sales and envelope stuffing
Endless meetings with minutes, treasury reports, and elections
Pushing a book cart in a hospital
Collecting money door to door for a local charity
Freedom to experiment with new interests and explore new areas
A bridge to paid employment
All of the above

If your attitude about volunteering your time leans toward the first four selections, you may be amazed to discover that today's volunteer is a new breed of woman with attitudes quite different from those many of us harbor from past generations. The image of a volunteer as a wealthy, sedate, white-gloved lady who raises funds for her pet charity is as outmoded as the horse and buggy. Today, volunteerism is an opportunity for women of every financial, educational, and social stratum to broaden and expand her horizon in any direction she may choose.

You're on the right road if you think that volunteerism is "all of the above." But do you know how many paths there are to explore? Paths that can lead you along byways that you may never have considered? Interviews with people who began their careers as volunteers or who are using the volunteer approach for their own special purposes may offer ideas that will open doors for you.

How many of us think of volunteering as something we *should* do? We *should* bake a cake to raise money for the needy. We *should* sell personalized umbrellas to aid our local hospital; we *should* sell candy for the PTA benefit. Certainly all these causes are worthwhile. Do you feel the things you *should* do are those that you really *want* to do? Are there some ways you could fulfill the needs of your community and your personal needs as well?

The answer? Yes!

Voluntary, according to Webster, means "done, made, given, undertaken, entered into of one's own free will, not forced or compelled." A volunteer, then, can do whatever he or she wishes. It is a free choice.

The scope of volunteer work is literally limitless. The choices are vast. A job that you *want* to do can be much more of a motivating aspect than a job you *should* do. The want and should jobs can be combined successfully and with good conscience.

EXPLORE A NEW YOU

Volunteer services are being utilized in so many ways and

with such great flexibility that a job can be almost tailored to the abilities, interests, and available time of the individual. A volunteer can easily use her time to explore new career possibilities and expand her potential, while serving a real need in the community.

Joan Blanford, age twenty-eight, is a perfect example. I talked to Joan, a former English teacher, in her New York City apartment while two-year-old Jamie napped. "It's hard to believe how much I've learned, the fun I've had and the people I've met during the past fifteen months. When we moved to New York, the baby was eight months old. I didn't know a soul other than my husband and the lady who rented us the apartment. I was miserable. I couldn't use my English teacher training as I was not registered to teach in New York, and I didn't want to leave the baby. My sister came to visit and she took a role acting in a local theater. I offered to write press releases for the play. Now look what's happened!" She pointed to a stack of mail, then interrupted our interview to answer the phone. When she hung up, she smiled broadly and said, "I feel like an executive."

Joan explained that writing a press release, typing it, and mailing it from home led to follow-up phone calls. She arranged radio and TV interviews for her sister, the playwright, and some of the production staff. The play took off and was a local hit. More important, it was stimulating for Joan. She could set her own working hours while the baby was asleep. When the play closed, Joan felt let down, lost. She looked for outlets for her newfound public relations talent.

Next, Joan phoned the Voluntary Action Line in her community and explained her experience. Was there anyone who needed her? They immediately had her contact several volunteer agencies who were eager to use her experience. Each group supplied Joan with basic background information and news of upcoming events. Joan wrote press releases and distributed them to the proper media sources. In only a few months, she had quite a scrapbook of published press releases. She has become acquainted with key media people in the community and knows she can count on them for references for a paying job she is eyeing in the future. One newspaper already asked her to write press releases on a part-time basis. Who knows what will open up in the future? Joan's whole life turned around once she offered to write the theater press releases, and she is grateful. "Elated," Joan corrected me. "It put me not only into the swim, but I feel like I'm leading, not treading water, not following, but being in control of my own direction. Discovering what I can do for me. And," she smiled, patting her protruding middle, "I can continue doing all of it after my second baby arrives."

TRY ON A CAREER

Volunteering can also let you try on a career. Often, what someone thinks would be the perfect outlet could easily be a failure. Volunteering can make you aware of the real time involvement and skills needed before you court failure. It can conceivably turn potential failure into real success.

Diane Arkan, the energetic mother of two preschoolers, delights in telling the story of her experience. "I hadn't realized all the busy work involved with what I thought was the utopian job. I learned that I had to stand back and re-evaluate my objectives. Luckily, the investment in time hadn't been great and I was able to learn early that the work wasn't for me."

She outlined that "Volunteering pinpointed several things I really wanted to do and eliminated those I didn't. It gave me the ability to experience different aspects of a variety of jobs through varying channels. It was exciting to discover *me* and what I could do without worrying about being fired or pleasing a boss."

Diane had volunteered to help with a survey of part-time jobs available for women in the area. That led to helping with survey work for a candidate's political campaign. Next she organized a fund-raising drive for a local hospital. "I never thought I had the ability to organize so many people, so many facets of the work. It went very well," she said proudly. "There were so many aspects to the campaign that it gave me insight into areas I could conceivably concentrate on later." For the present Diane felt she was helping the community and herself while having ample time to spend with her children.

Carol Connors was surrounded by ledgers and green-lined pages when I interviewed her in the office of a hospital gift shop in Philadelphia. "I always thought I'd like to own a gift shop," she peered over her glasses. "Right now I don't have the money or the time because I have a sixteen-month-old son. But, wow! What I've learned working here at the hospital gift shop two mornings a week! I could never have learned all the practical aspects of running a business in three years of college merchandising courses. I didn't know a ledger page from a recipe. There's so much more to know about buying and selling and what will make a profit than what I had naively thought was involved. Now I'm taking a course in accounting one night a week while my husband minds the baby. Next semester I've signed up for marketing."

Carol may or may not eventually open a gift shop, but she is certainly preparing herself for a goal and expanding her knowledge.

STEP OUT TO PAID EMPLOYMENT

Janet Kahn's volunteer job brought her a stimulating paid career. As a volunteer for the Junior League, she served on a committee to study how public school buildings could be used by the entire community after regular school hours. A decision to establish evening adult education classes was made. Janet entered into a volunteer position as the Junior League's representative (they were funding a major portion of the project) to create programs and hire teachers for a large segment of the adult education classes in the community.

Thanks to political machinations, two part-time salaried positions were established; Janet moved from volunteer to part-time paid administrator for a program entitled LEAP: Lifetime Education for All Persons. "I was really in the right place at the right time. I don't think an opportunity like this one would come up in a lifetime if I were looking for it. I never expected to fall into a paid job. My general philosophy about volunteering had always been that in order to take from a community, you should give your time in return. This job has been great. I've met so many people in the community, I have a real sense of accomplishment. I set my own hours, so I have ample time for my children, my most important priority."

Volunteering can definitely help you get a foot in the door to paid employment. I spoke to Wendy Altwin, a thirty-year-old law school graduate who became a mother before she had a chance to practice law. Wendy emphasized the importance of thinking ahead through volunteer jobs. She said, "When I graduated, I pounded the pavement looking for jobs and was greeted by the old cliche, 'We're looking for someone with experience.' But how do you get that experience unless someone gives you a job first? The answer for me now is by volunteering. I'm getting experience in many facets of people's legal problems. When I am ready for the job market, I can skip that bottom rung in a law office. I'm still keeping up with current legal trends and have ample time with my fifteen-month-old son. It's the best of both worlds for me at this stage of my life."

MAINTAIN YOUR SKILLS

Many women are discovering that volunteer work is also a marvelous opportunity for maintaining skills that could become dull if not kept sharp. When you cannot work for pay, volunteering should be considered a way to keep on top of your field without a large time commitment.

Barbara Cahan does just that. "I'm twenty-eight," she said, "and I hold a graduate degree in social work. I have four years of on-the-job experience; some of that includes seven and a half months after Melissa was born. That means the baby was in a nursery under other people's care for much of those early months. I began to feel I was missing out on the fun of mothering." Barbara mused a little, then added, "Not only did I yearn to spend more time with the baby, I felt I wasn't practicing what I was preaching. I wanted to be more responsible for my child's upbringing during the formative years. Yet, I didn't want to lose touch with the counseling I had always enjoyed."

What was Barbara's solution? A volunteer position. After some investigation among the social service agencies in the Dallas suburb near her home, Barbara was able to line up work two mornings a week with a few select clients. It was exactly what she wanted and needed. "When I'm ready to return to a full-time job, I will be more aware of changes in the field and I'll have up-to-date references for another position," she predicted.

CONTRIBUTE TO PERSONAL GROWTH

As a volunteer, a woman can make societal contributions while fostering her own psychological growth. Women who have never envisioned themselves as jobholders, leaders, or innovators often function and grow in these positions. They gain confidence in themselves and strengthen their personalities.

When Sheila Barnes said, "I had always considered myself a shy person," I did a double take. Sheila was thirty-two; her posture and her movements exuded confidence and poise. I pointed this out. Sheila confessed that it was all learned over a period of three years and much of it was through organization work. "My mother was always involved in a fund-raising group, which mixed civic activities and camaraderie. When I moved to Atlanta I joined the local chapter of the same group, mainly to meet people. I was home with two small babies in a strange city and felt sorry for myself. Soon the meetings became the highlight of my weeks. I looked forward to my evening out, to phone calls from other women to help out with this or that. I felt needed, wanted, and that someone besides my husband and pediatrician knew I existed."

Sheila's husband, who participated in the interview, quickly nodded in agreement, recalling those few trying months in the new city.

Her enthusiasm warmed the room as she continued. "What was thrilling for me was that I could become so excited about some of the group's activities. I had always thought of myself as a follower, but soon I was the chairwoman of two committees. Within a year and a half, I was president of the organization. I was delegating responsibility, working well and harmoniously with many people, interrelating our group's role with city committees, and so forth. I even traveled to a national meeting in Boston! It was marvelous. I gained a new confidence and a new insight into *me*."

THE CAUSE IS THE COMMITMENT

Many people volunteer hundreds of helpful hours in areas where specific services benefited them or members of their family.

A woman who had been raised in New York's inner-city Harlem area told me that her younger brother had had a serious drug problem when he was fourteen and was heading for trouble. The local drug rehabilitation agency did wonders for him. "I wanted to give my time to try to help others avert a tragic life," she said. "I went through the agency's training programs. Now my number is available for a hotline two evenings a week and I hope to give more time as I can."

Another woman explained, "My grandmother enjoys the county senior citizens' program so much I decided to help with programming. My job is to find speakers and people to teach classes. Most of the contacts can be made from home during Lauren's nap time so I don't feel I'm taking time away from her. I've met many interesting people who have a variety and wealth of life experience. The senior citizens are very appreciative. And, when I go to the group's program with the baby, it's as though she has forty grandparents. They love it and she responds to all of the attention."

SCOUT THE VOLUNTEER JOB SCENE

How and where do you learn about volunteer opportunities in your area? Begin by calling the Voluntary Action Line in your community. Its number is listed in the telephone book's white pages under Volunteers or Volunteer Clearing House, or a similar listing. If you are unable to find the local agency, write to the National Center for Voluntary Action, 1214 16th St. N.W., Washington, DC 20036. Ask for the Voluntary Action Center in your area.

Opportunities for volunteer services are often listed in the newspapers. If not, phone your newspaper office and ask if such a listing is available. It may take a few phone calls and connections with different people, but you should generate an answer. If none exists, you might stimulate such a column in your newspaper. Volunteer to write it, and you are started on a newspaper career!

The *Washington Post* lists volunteer opportunities each Saturday in a column headed Ann's Reader Exchange. Some of the listings look like great fun and perform an essential service. They include teaching handicapped children to ride horses, researching historical places in the area, teaching crafts at a senior citizens' center, and learning to perform puppet shows at a children's hospital. The requests change each week.

A friend in San Diego sent in a story from that city's newspaper requesting volunteers who can speak Spanish and English to work as receptionists in dental clinics, hospitals, and a children's school. What a marvelous way to keep a second language brushed up!

You local church or synagogue can clue you in to religious organizations that may be able to use your services.

The League of Women Voters has a wide variety of interesting, worthwhile, and stimulating projects. They sponsor programs dealing with the environment, women's rights, mass transit, trade and aid, police services, congress and the president, health care delivery, education, day care, world hunger, voting rights, and others. Select the time you can help and allow your voice to make an impact on any of these issues. You will find a local chapter of the League of Women Voters listed in the telephone book's white pages. If there is no listing, you may wish to help charter a chapter. For information, contact League of Women Voters of the United States, 1730 M St. N.W., Washington, DC 20036.

College and university directors are recognizing the advantages and skills a person can acquire through volunteer jobs. Many college programs now offer course credit for volunteer experiences. There is abundant information about this recent development in a booklet titled *How to Get College Credit for What You Have Learned as a Homemaker and Volunteer.* See chapter 12 for a detailed report about this booklet and its availability.

Choose your volunteer job by the same standards you would apply in seeking paid employment. Go about it in a conscientious, professional, businesslike manner.

If you are making an effort to do a volunteer job, for whatever purpose, that job should be worth the same effort it might take to hold a paying job. Actually, the volunteer job should be even more satisfying and fill your prescribed requirements, because you are not being paid for it monetarily. Contacts, friendships, and emotional outlet may be the only payment you need at this point.

FLEXIBILITY: THE GIANT PLUS

The fact that volunteer work allows you to do as much or

as little as you like is so obvious that it is sometimes overlooked as one of the giant plus factors. You can make a commitment of one morning a week for two hours if that's what you find available for your own goals. Perhaps that is all the time you can spare while your child is in play groups. Maybe you can increase it to two mornings a week once he or she is in nursery school. You can volunteer your time at home during a child's nap time, or in the evenings. You don't necessarily have to incur the cost of sitters or long automobile commutes to and from a job. You can take vacations when you want and stay home if your children are sick. You can switch projects.

Use volunteering as a testing ground. How will returning to work be compatible with your family life? A short volunteer work load that increases gradually may be a good way to ease into a longer time commitment in a job with pay.

The most important aspect about volunteering is that you are involved. Involved with broadening your scope beyond your home. Involved with doing something for *you*.

A word of caution: the fact that volunteering is so flexible does not mean you can take your commitment lightly. If you sign on to do a job, do it. Be reliable and dependable. It's always a good habit to form.

Young mothers who are involved in a variety of volunteer programs agree that volunteerism is a marvelous way to enrich their lives and that of others. The opportunities are unlimited. They can lead to the development of a new career or interest, help maintain skills, or enhance personal development. Volunteering allows you to expand your outlook while still permitting ample time for your home and family.

12

Back to School?

While I was pregnant with Jordan we learned we would be moving to Washington, D.C. the following year. My husband was offered positions at several universities. All things being equal, we chose the Washington, D.C., area because the University of Maryland offered a graduate program in communications for me.

Before the baby was born I recognized that I had to have some goal beyond child rearing. Graduate school was my answer. At the time I didn't think any other choices would be open when we moved. I assumed I would qualify as a part-time student. I had graduated from college with honors and had several years of job experience in the communications field.

I reviewed the application. It asked for my grade point average. No problem. But what about my GRE scores and letters of recommendation from three professors? I laughed with tears in my eyes. College seemed like yesterday and yet it had been seven years since I had been a student. I vaguely recalled taking the Graduate Record Exams, but I had had no intention of going for a master's degree then. I couldn't remember the names of most of my professors. How could I expect them to remember me? How many of the same profs were still at the same university teaching the same courses? I sent the letter-of-recommendation form to one professor. Old employers? I phoned the advertising agencies I had worked for; as I had suspected, the staff had changed and my immediate bosses had moved on to other companies. The people I finally asked to write letters probably drummed up sentences as stale as my now yellowing diploma.

I submitted the application and waited anxiously. Finally the envelope arrived. I tore it open, wondering when my registration day would be. Instead, staring at me was a big fat rejection that noted "low GRE test scores."

It was a stunning blow to my ego.

Two years later I appeared on the campus of the University of Maryland, not as a student but in the office of the Returning Women's Counseling Center. Had I not been researching material for this book, I probably would have been unaware of this office or similar services that are blossoming at colleges and universities throughout the country.

Many things have changed since my college days; the days of Viet Nam, when college and university admissions offices were overflowing with students who wanted to go to school. After the war ended, the populations within the ivy-covered halls dwindled, and school administrators began to search for ways to lure adults into their learning web with special services.

The women's movement began to gain ground at the same time. Women's study programs mushroomed throughout the country. Awareness of women and the special needs of adult women returning to school began to grow.

At the University of Maryland, two counselors, Beverly Greenfieg and Barbara Goldberg, observed that an increasing number of returning women came to the reading and study skills lab for counseling and advising. The counselors recognized that almost all of the women verbalized common concerns: lack of up-to-date study skills; feelings of isolation on the campus because of their age (yes, twenty-seven is considered old); conflicts related to fulfilling multiple roles as wives, mothers, students; and lack of clarity and/or information regarding their academic and vocational goals.

How did the counselors respond?

First, they established a support group for women students to share their common problems. Special courses, workshops, seminars, and counseling evolved from the shared ideas in this original group. Free workshops on goal setting, study skills, and careers were offered to the community.

I sat in on some of these sessions. I noticed a feeling of camaraderie, a lifeline, a sincere sense of belonging among the returning women. They had a refuge on this huge campus. With thousands of students, here was a place where their special problems were resolved.

Support groups, counseling, and new programs for women are among a multitude of services available to ease your return to campus. First you must know what you want and how to achieve it.

RETURNING WOMEN'S COUNSELING SERVICES

How do you plan to return to school? Do you decide on a major and apply? Do you take a course and try on the college experience?

Locate your school's counseling center. Explain your situation to the secretary; that you are a mature woman interested in returning to school. Ask if there is a particular counselor who deals with women such as yourself. Don't be vague and say, "I'd like to make an appointment with a counselor." Assert yourself. This is of major importance to you. To keep the appointment you will need to arrange for a sitter, locate the building and counseling office, find a place to park. You are not an eighteen-year-old who cannot decide whether to take a history seminar this semester or next. Make sure you get exactly what you want. Your time is valuable.

You've made the appointment. You've arranged for a sitter. What can you expect from a university counselor?

The counselor will help you evaluate where you are right now, and try to verbalize your specific needs. She will probably emphasize the need to explore many areas, by taking one course or by attending a workshop. She might suggest a counseling center that stresses career counseling. She may have you take a vocational test. She may answer questions about admissions and help you fill out an application.

A counselor will *not* give you a cut and dried answer to all of your problems. She is there to help you explore available possibilities. Most counselors I talked to asked me to emphasize this point: Don't feel you have to have specific questions or goals when you walk in for counseling. It's OK to say, "I'm twenty-nine years old and I don't know what to do with the rest of my life." It's even OK to say, "I don't know what I want to be when I grow up," because most people don't.

When I spoke to Beverly Greenfeig at the University of Maryland about my specific problem—low GRE scores, and very old and vaguely reliable references, she explained how the reading and study skills lab could help me. She suggested I listen to a tape on how to score higher on standardized exams. She pointed out a course given within the continuing education division on how to take the GRE exams.

"What about my references?" I asked. She explained that the counseling center is attuned to professors who are sympathetic to returning women students. I could enroll in one credit course as a special student to prove my abilities to the particular division. This would serve two important purposes. I would have a course under my belt, and, assuming I did well, I could ask for a recommendation from that professor to the department head in my subject area.

She also told me of a one-credit course entitled College Aims for Returning Women that included assistance in choosing a major, any necessary academic advice, career planning and vocational testing, reading and study skills, and how to organize time effectively. This would be another way to get a recommendation from an up-to-date resource.

The reading and study skills lab was a revelation. I listened to interesting, well-prepared tapes on how to take lecture notes, listening competency, effective reading, grammar, how to study, and how to take a test—to list a few. What a terrific tool for the returning woman student whose reading and study skills are rusty! And, with the tapes, you can listen over and over again until you digest and assimilate the information you need.

If you are already certain about your educational goals, it's still to your advantage to meet with a counselor. So many aspects of education have probably changed since you were on campus that a counselor might be able to shed additional information on your return. She may help you become aware of recent job possibilities in your field. A counselor is sensitive to your needs. Use her as a resource. If she is only able to point you to university services you may be able to use, it's worth it. One hint is enough to warrant the time and effort, but a counselor may be an endless source. Even a note on the office bulletin board may be the one piece of information for which you have been searching.

Whenever you decide to see a counselor or take a course, be a consumer! If a state university offers free counseling and a private college charges a fee, where are you likely to go? Some private colleges claim they can be more innovative because they don't have to go through state and federal bureaucracies, but try the free programs first. You may get exactly what you need.

NEW DIMENSIONS IN WOMEN'S PROGRAMS

Programs similar to the counseling service at the University of Maryland are sprouting throughout the country. They are not limited to large universities in big cities. There are many different types of programs available today. I feel it is important to be aware of as many as possible, so you will have an idea of what to look for in your community. The new directions and results of these programs for women are eye opening!

Higher learning centers are instituting ideas to make the college experience meaningful for women in today's society. How many of us felt culture shock when our first job after school showed us how little our education had prepared us for our careers!

Educators have found that on-the-job training can increase the awareness of the real-world employment situation. Paid internships at colleges like Mills in Oakland, California, and the University of Kentucky in Lexington are a new step toward integration of education and career.

Centers similar to Mills' Career and Life Planning Center also are a plus to women interested in making their education more practical. This marvelous center includes a resource library, personal counseling, panel and group discussions that focus on preparation for specific careers, information on graduate school requirements, and workshops on writing resumes, job interviewing, and other placement techniques. A lecture series featuring women professionals as role models has also been successful.

Perhaps the course of study that you need is not available in your city's college or university, or you live in an area without a higher learning institution. A nonresidential program may be your answer. Nonresidential programs are a boon to the mother who wants to stay at home and earn a degree. The adult degree program at Mary Baldwin College in Staunton, Virginia, is an example. It is designed so a student may work independently at her own pace and at the location that best suits her study plan and life circumstances.

You are interested in pursuing a career, but one subject is holding you back. Is that subject math? You are not alone. In fact, so many women have a problem with math that a new phrase has been coined—math anxiety. Educators noticed that women are concentrated in a few major occupations—those not requiring a math background. Women are frequently locked out of scientific and technical careers, even quantitative work in the social sciences, due to poor preparation in math.

Because of a lack of mathematical skills, women do not have the same options in careers as men. At the University of

Washington in Seattle, four years of high school math are required for admission to eleven of the sixteen major fields of undergraduate studies. In the 1976 entering freshman class only 28 percent of the females, compared to 51 percent of the males, had taken four years of high school math.

The University of Washington established a program to help women overcome this anxiety. Rather than attempt to improve students' math ability through remedial training, often a negative association, the program proposed to increase math ability through spatial visualization. Counselors also help students explore sexual stereotypes and social expectations as they have influenced their attitudes toward math. In addition, students are taught to identify and manage their own anxiety as it affects their performance.

Math anxiety workshops and classes are available in many university adult education programs all over the country. If you have a problem with math, overcoming it may open up many new career options for you.

Recognition of prior learning is another phenomenon in education that has stemmed from the return of women to college. Women who have had extensive experience in volunteer or other work have demonstrated their competencies as a basis for obtaining college credit. *How to Get College Credit for What You Have Learned as a Homemaker and Volunteer* is a workbook designed to help re-entry women evaluate the skills they have utilized in homemaking and volunteer work. It details the process involved in getting accreditation within a variety of academic institutions. Chapters include information about different kinds of experiences re-entry women may have had and the skills acquired from them, information colleges may require before granting credit for homemaking and volunteer experiences, costs that may be involved in trying to obtain credits, and problems and difficulties that may be encountered. The workbook is available for $3 through Ruth B. Ekstrom, Educational Testing Service, Princeton, NJ 08541.

Communities have recognized the importance of adult women's education. WYES, public television in New Orleans, is providing information to women through a television series of monthly, live, sixty-minute programs that offer information to potential women students. These programs deal with the locations and curricular offerings of postsecondary educational institutions; the financial implications of returning to school or college; coping with feelings of inadequacy and insecurity, especially for older women who have been out of school for years; advice on how to handle family adjustments, child care; special problems of displaced homemakers and Spanish-speaking women.

To complement the information given on the program, a directory of area postsecondary institutions is provided free of charge, along with a resource sheet printed with names and agencies referred to on each program. Further outreach is achieved when opportunity representatives speak before interested organizations and use videotapes of the programs.

How about learning a language over the telephone? The Community CTC (Classroom Telephone Computer) at the University of Michigan in Ann Arbor delivers instruction in math, language, logic, scientific method, and reasoning by telephone to anyone in the community. Education is at the convenience and pace of the learner rather than those of the institution, delivered over the telephone in the comfort of your own home. Learning French during your child's nap time *has* to be better than watching the soaps!

Flexibility in class scheduling is another noticeable change in education. Weekend and evening courses are advantageous to the mother who can rely on sitters or husband to a greater degree than she can during the day. The University of Maryland's University College offers courses in arts, business, economics, education, government, and sociology, which you can complete in only seven weeks of intensive study. Classes are easier to get to, often held in branch buildings throughout the community to offer adults easier access to courses.

Re-entry women have their own college "sorority" today. It's called Peer Counseling. You are assigned a sort of big sister who is already in the program to guide you through your college experiences. Imagine how great it will be to have someone your age to talk to who has made the adjustment you are facing. You have an immediate friend and confidante from the day you begin that first class.

As you can see, there are a multitude of programs helpful to women interested in returning to school. How do you choose the right one for you? A new service for student consumers is the education broker. Services like the Regional Learning Service Project in Syracuse, New York, match students' needs with the most appropriate postsecondary educational activity or, in some cases, suggest alternatives to formal education. Fees are charged on a sliding scale according to income. When you think about it, you could waste a lot of time and money in a program that is not quite right for you because you were unaware of what others might offer. An education broker may be of great help.

CAN I DO IT? YES!

These days programs for women are phenomenal. The important thing to realize is that colleges and universities are bending over backward to get you, the returning women, into their programs. Studies have shown that returning adult women are among the most highly motivated students on campus. They are more mature, they have worked in a variety of jobs with differing experiences, and they are more disciplined. You know that you have a clearer view of what you want out of life than you had when you were eighteen. You have a more solid purpose. Your concerns are different. So much of prior university life is taken up with social matters.

That's all very nice, of course, but I'm sure you are wondering about some basic apprehensions; namely, how do I make time for studying, afford the tuition, and if I'm putting all of this energy and money into school, how can I get less than an A?

The best advice from women who have returned to school is to start *slowly*. Take only one course during the first semester, one with which you feel you might have the most success. Don't punish yourself by taking the most difficult course in your curriculum or overloading yourself with so much work that you might fail. You don't begin an exercise program without warming up and gradually increasing your stamina; think of going to school in the same way. Test your best study hours—your child's nap time, the evenings, etc. One woman leaves her two-year-old at the university day care center two full days a week. She has two classes in the morning and spends the afternoon studying in the library. If she finishes early, she picks up her child early or uses the time to accomplish other things. Papers, research, and reading are done for the most part during those two afternoons.

Yes, I know that you want to get an A in every course you take, but how crucial is it? Most important is that you are working toward your goal. When you seek a job no one will ask you what your grades were. The education is the key; everything beyond that is what you do with the opportunities that come your way.

Be prepared for the classes you miss if your child is ill. Make friends with someone in the class whose notes you can borrow in an emergency, or if your family takes a vacation during class time. Know people you can count on if your sitter gets sick. Be prepared! Be confident!

Good luck, coed!

FINANCIAL RESOURCES

The escalating costs of education are real. If you are in need of financial aid to continue your studies, write to the following sources for information on scholarships, fellowships, or loans.

Financial Aid: Where to Get It and How to Use It

Business & Professional Women's Foundation,
Scholarship Department
2012 Massachusetts Ave. N.W.
Washington, DC 20036

Financial Aid: A Partial List of Resources for Women

Project on the Status and Education of Women
Association of American Colleges
1818 R St. N.W.
Washington, DC 20009

A Guide to Selected Fellowships, Scholarships and Internships in Higher Education ($1 postpaid)

American Association of University Women
2401 Virginia Ave. N.W.
Washington, DC 20037

Selected List of Post-secondary Opportunities for Minorities and Women

Bureau of Higher and Continuing Education
U.S. Office of Education
400 Maryland Ave. S.W.
Washington, DC 20037

A Selected List of Major Fellowship Opportunities and Aids to Advanced Education for United States Citizens

Publications Officer
National Science Foundation
1800 G St. N.W.
Washington, DC 20550

Student Consumer's Guide

Six Federal Financial Aid Programs
Department of Health, Education & Welfare
P.O. Box 84
Washington, DC 20044

Altrusa International Foundation

Provides awards to women for training or retraining to qualify for employment. Emphasis on vocational education—nursing, X-ray tech, bookkeeping—rather than college degree.

Chairman, Founders Fund Vocational Aid Committee
Altrusa International Foundation, Inc.
332 South Michigan Ave.
Chicago, IL 60604

American Association of University Women

Awards dissertation fellowships to women who have completed all course work and qualifying examinations in a doctoral program. Also offers graduate fellowships to foreign women planning to return to their native countries to pursue careers.

Director, AAUW Educational Foundation Programs
2401 Virginia Ave. N.W.
Washington, DC 20037

Association for Women's Active Return to Education (AWARE) Scholarships

Modest scholarships to full- or part-time students over age twenty-five who are returning to college after an absence; applicable only at selected colleges in California, Arizona, and Texas.

Dr. Revena Jacobsen
5820 Wilshire Blvd.
Los Angeles, CA 90037

Business and Professional Women's Foundation

Awards career advancement scholarships to adult women

who need further training or education to begin careers or to improve professional opportunities. Scholarships are based on financial need for women twenty-five and over who are returning for vocational training, undergraduate, or graduate work after a break in their education. Graduate fellowships are also available for doctoral candidates. Deadlines: May 1 and October 1.

Business and Professional Women's Foundation
2012 Massachusetts Ave. N.W.
Washington, DC 20036

Clairol Loving Care Scholarship Program

The Clairol Program is the only nationwide company-sponsored fund for women of age thirty and older who are continuing postsecondary educations to achieve career goals. Scholarships are available for full- or part-time study in vocational schools, undergraduate college degree programs, or graduate work at the Master's or professional level.

Ellen Anderson, Administrator
Clairol Loving Care Scholarship Program
345 Park Ave., 5th Floor
New York, NY 10022
(212) 644-3020

Danforth Graduate Fellowship Program—Early Entry Program

For persons graduating from college and entering graduate education. Late Entry Program for postbaccalaureate students returning to graduate education after a break, or in graduate school at the time of application.

The Danforth Foundation
222 South Central Ave.
St. Louis, MO 63105
(314) 862-6200

Diuguid Fellowship Program

Administered by the Council of Southern Universities; makes funds available to mature women. Consideration is given to women whose career and professional goals have been deferred because of marriage, children, etc. Applicants must live in the South.

Executive Director
Council of Southern Universities, Inc.
795 Peachtree St. N.E.
Suite 484
Atlanta, GA 30308

Florence Morse Scholarship

Awarded to women at least twenty-five years of age who are United States citizens and are in their junior or senior year of a business course accredited by the American Assembly of Collegiate Schools of Business. Deadlines: May 1 and October 1.

William Laidlaw, Jr., Managing Director
Florence Morse Scholarship
760 Office Parkway
Suite 50
St. Louis, MO 63141

General Federation of Women's Clubs

In the past two years approximately $2.5 million has been awarded to women through local and state chapters of women's clubs. For further information contact the president of the women's club in your community. (If you have trouble finding a listing, contact the chamber of commerce to determine the name of the local club.)

George R. and Eliza Gardner Howard Foundation

Fellowships for individuals ages thirty to forty years old

who pursue studies in the fields of languages and literature, social sciences, history, philosophy, and fine, applied, and performing arts.

George R. and Eliza Gardner Howard Foundation
Box 1867
Brown University
Providence, RI 02912

PEO

Assists mature returning women students.

Ms. Florence Myers Wallace, Chairman
PEO Continuing Education
3700 Grant Ave.
Des Moines, IA 50312

Philip Morris Scholarship Fund

Provides funds to women twenty-five and older who are engaged in part-time only undergraduate study at either community or four-year colleges.

Sears-Roebuck Foundation

Beginning in the fall of 1975, this organization made $300,000 available in loan funds to women of any age who had been accepted for graduate degree programs or graduate-level courses of study at schools accredited on the graduate level by the American Assembly of Collegiate Schools of Business. Women may qualify for individual loans. Repayment of loans is scheduled over a five-year period with low interest beginning one year after graduation.

Business and Professional Women's Foundation
2012 Massachusetts Ave. N.W.
Washington, DC 20036

Second Career Scholarships for Displaced Homemakers

Funding for counseling to assess the displaced homemaker's needs and skills, and for job retraining.

Business and Professional Women's Foundation
2012 Massachusetts Ave. N.W.
Washington, DC 20036

Soroptimist Awards

Training awards to assist mature women to enter or re-enter the labor market.

Soroptimists International
1616 Walnut St.
Philadelphia, PA 19103

Sororia Alumnae Scholarships

Provides low-cost residence, grants, loans, and scholarships to women returning to school.

The Sororia Alumnae
University of Washington
1603 N.E. Ravenna Blvd.
Spokane, WA 98105

Contact the financial aid director of the school you want to attend. Inquire about sources of assistance, including national defense student loans. Borrowing the necessary money may be an investment in your future.

Contact women's organizations in your community and state. Many have some kind of assistance program for students that may be available to the mature or part-time student. Don't forget the women's service clubs such as Altrusa, Zonta, Quota, Soroptimist, and Pilot.

Is there a professional organization in your vocational area? If so, get in touch with the local president and explain your educational plans and your financial need. Perhaps one of their projects could aid your situation.

13

Back to Work?

Returning to work is a very personal, individual decision. For some women there is no choice; their families cannot survive financially on only one income. For others there is a choice.

TO WORK OR NOT TO WORK . . .

Plenty of people around you will offer opinions about when, how, and why you should or should not work once you're a mother. Your first decision will be how to handle all the unasked-for free advice. When you are secure in this important decision and do decide to go back to a job, things have a way of falling into place. This may not be as easy as it sounds, of course. Feeling right includes being certain your child has the proper mother substitute, having solid support from your husband, and gaining self-satisfaction and stimulation from your job. Having all these priorities in the proper order will give you the confidence you need to close the door behind you and go off to work.

How readily can you do that? How can you shut out your home responsibilities and concentrate solely on your job? It's not easy. Not nearly as easy for a mother as for a father, explained several women.

"It seems I can never leave everything behind," sighed Nancy Coleman, who works as a loan officer. "I always worry that I forgot to tell the sitter something, what to make for dinner, if I dressed Benjamin warmly enough. My husband doesn't worry about these things. He goes off to work and when he gets home, dinner is ready and the baby looks taken care of."

. . . OR WHEN

Rebecca Young wrestled with the question of separation between herself and her baby. She was unsure when the best time would be to go back to the job.

"I worried about leaving Jenny. I enjoyed being home with her. My boss phoned often and asked when I would return. His temporary secretary only wanted to stay on another month. Finally, I decided that I would just do it, because we really needed the money and I was beginning to feel guilty about the time I was sitting home and not working."

When to leave your child is one of the most difficult decisions you will have to make. Optimally, it's best to wait until all your children are safely packed off to school. That may be quite a few years off. Postponing self-fulfillment and monetary needs until that day may seem illogical and impossible.

In my interviews with working mothers, pediatricians, and child psychologists, there was a consensus that the next easiest time to leave a child is in infancy. From the start, the child is brought up and conditioned that mommy and daddy leave and always come home. The child has a sense of order and is aware of all his caretakers from the beginning.

"My infant napped most of the day," related one working mother. "I had planned to stay home and be very motherly, but the baby slept so much during those early months that I felt I was needed only to provide food and change diapers. My job was flexible, so I decided to work. At three months, Michael is awake about three hours or so with the sitter. His other awake hours are in the early morning until his 9 A.M. nap and from 4 to 7 P.M. These are with me or my husband.

It is probably most difficult to leave a child when he is a toddler. He has been home with mommy daily for more than a year. Separation at that point can be difficult for both mother and child.

THE EIGHTEEN-HOUR STRESS TEST

Fatigue rears its ugly head as a major frustration among working mothers. Many soon realize, as one mother expressed it, "I don't work an eight-hour day; I work an eighteen-hour day!"

The working mother's fatigue is so well recognized by physicians that it is medically known as asthenic housewife syndrome. Physicians can quickly pinpoint this malady when they hear the complaint, "I'm exhausted! I never feel well!"

"And it's no wonder," said one physician, who practices general internal medicine. "When I ask these women to describe their typical day, it's incredible. I suggest they actually write down what they do in any one day. Once their activities face them on paper, they begin to understand why they are tired, why they imagine a variety of disorders. Often, in addition to being so exhausted and overtired, they don't sleep well. We evaluate different parts of the day, and I suggest alternatives to alleviate some of the stress.

"Of course, there is the occasional woman who does have some kind of physical or mental disorder that needs treatment. It is a good idea to see your doctor in case of undue anxiety, stress, depression, or other physical or mental problems.

Simple treatment may be all you need. We always like to be sure, however."

Stress and anxiety are a part of every working mother's day. However, to many women, the psychological benefits, the accomplishments, and the stimulation of a job are compensation for the heavy work load.

"When the novelty of the baby wore off after the first few months, Chuck would ask me daily what I had done. My daily response was, 'nurse, burp, diaper the baby and clean the house.' When I took walk after walk with the baby, I realized that I was frustrated. Chuck and I had little to talk about. He always had reports of his business transactions and I soon realized dinner conversations were a monologue. I had nothing to talk about. I felt dull, bored, and boring. Now that I am working again I feel like a more vital person. We are more the equal couple we were before the baby. We feel we are contributing together to the well-being of the total family relationship. It really has made a difference in my marriage and my mothering."

THE WORKING COUPLE

A supportive, cooperative, interested husband is a major plus for the working mother, and more husbands assume this role today than in the past. Heartwarming comments I heard include the following.

"I rarely have to ask my husband for help. He pitches in and does his share, sometimes even more!"

"We feel that housework, child care, shopping, etc., are both of our responsibilities. There are no 'womanly' duties."

"We both work; we both take care of the home. Some days it's more convenient for Jack to pick up the baby and start dinner, while I stop at the grocery store, the cleaner, whatever."

"We are a team."

"We know what has to get done and we do it."

"We stress our leisure time, and the work is done more quickly because our other goals are much more important."

All husbands and wives have to work out home management to the best of their abilities. The most efficient way to split jobs is to decide who is best at what.

"My husband is a lousy, slow cook who uses every pot, pan, and utensil in sight just to make a tuna fish sandwich," mused Eileen Grady, who works as a guidance counselor. "So I opt to do the cooking. I never suggest that 'I cooked tonight; tomorrow it's your turn.' It doesn't help. I pick the baby up from the sitter and Joel takes over her care while I make dinner. I put the baby to bed while he cleans the kitchen, takes out the garbage, and starts a load of laundry. Then we have time to relax and chat about our day."

Certainly many husbands are already carrying a heavy work load, long hours, and their own set of stresses. It may be difficult for them to help when they are needed. Or, your idea of help may differ from your husband's. The best tack is to sit down and explain rationally the needs of the household. Together you can work out solutions.

FINDING QUALITY TIME WITH YOUR CHILDREN

Through all of the juggling, arrangement, and fatigue, the most important consideration is your child. Could anyone sincerely justify holding a job if she misses out on her baby's development? Her child's first step? Holding and loving?

How do working mothers find quality time to spend with their children?

The wildest part of the day for any working mother is the morning, according to the mothers that I interviewed. The baby is dressed and ready for drop-off at the care center and suddenly he needs a diaper change. Your three-year-old spills juice on her dress. Now your outfit has some of the fallout—a spot on the front—and you didn't get the other blouse into the laundry the night before. These joys add to the already hectic routine of making sure that everyone is fed and cleaned, there's gas in the car, all the windows are closed, and there are notes for whoever requires them.

In spite of the A.M. chaos, every morning thousands of mothers seem to pull it all off, pull through and smile, spend precious special moments with their families, and greet the public as well.

Marion Johnson, working mother of a four-year-old and an eighteen-month-old, explains, "I allow extra time in the morning because I believe strongly in the family starting the day off with a nourishing breakfast together in a civilized fashion. It sets the pace of the day with a feeling of security and togetherness for everyone."

"My toddler is an early riser," notes Gloria Campanella, the bookkeeper for a chain of shoe stores. "Rather than trying desperately to sleep through those precious moments until 7 A.M., we begin our family day in our bed, playing and enjoying each other. Now that Erica sleeps in a big-girl bed, she gets up and crawls in with us—she's a bright way to begin the day."

An executive in a women's bank lives a mile from work and has office hours from 9:00 to 3:30. "I walk to work with Matthew in the stroller and pick him up on the way home. That way, I get my exercise, too. We can shop on the way home. There's a small playground in our apartment complex and, time and weather permitting, we swing and play before or after work."

"Driving Roger to nursery school has become a learning time. We sing songs, work on the alphabet, and turn the ten-minute drive into more than transportation."

Carol Collings, who lives in New York City, takes the bus with her son Ryan on the way to the day care center, which is within walking distance of her job. "The bus ride is fun for both of us. Ryan is beginning to talk. We identify objects, colors, animals. It's a togetherness time I always enjoy. And, a mamma and baby always manage to get a seat!"

Evenings, too, need to be arranged to make time for children.

"When I get home I give the baby a piece of fruit or a carrot to munch on to hold her off until dinner. I pour myself a cold drink or a glass of wine and we relax and play together for half an hour. Then I'm revitalized and can make the physical and mental switch from office to meal making. Rick usually gets home after the baby's supper and we all have play time together. He may bathe the baby while I prepare our dinner. One of us will read her a story. Once she's in bed we can have a leisurely dinner and the evening for ourselves."

Angie Garcia was adamant when she said, "Television was our nemesis and we quickly fell into a bad habit. Al and I would turn on the news and wait for Krista to fall asleep. Then we'd transfer her to her crib. When we realized that the newscaster was more familiar to us than our daughter, we revised our schedules. Now we read stories with the baby or work quietly on a puzzle before her bedtime. We try to catch the ten o'clock news, though I'm quite often fast asleep by then!"

NEW WAYS TO WORK

Perhaps you have mixed emotions or guilt feelings about combining motherhood with a career, but the income is essential or you need the stimulation. Maybe your attitude about working needs to be examined.

Work need not mean the typical nine-to-five job as we know it. Part of my approach for the working mother is to explore new ways to work, ways through which you as a mother can enjoy the best of all worlds—job stimulation, income, your baby, your home, your husband, and yourself. Going back to work doesn't have to mean the traditional rearrangement of your lifestyle and everyone's around you to fit society's eight-hour decree of what it means to hold down a job.

This book is written for you. Let's face it. Why did you

have a baby in the first place? Certainly not to walk out and hand her over to someone else. If it is a necessity, again, you have little choice. But, if the choice is yours to make, at least for the child's formative first year of life, here are some solid avenues to explore.

Part-Time Careers

If your idea of part-time employment is what you glean from that section of the classifieds, be happy to know that part-time work is more than being a go-go dancer, telephone sales person, or delivery person. The part-time career is an up and coming working phenomenon, and everyone, up to the President of the United States, is recognizing its importance in the structure of the labor force.

On October 10, 1978, President Jimmy Carter signed the Federal Employees Part-Time Career Employment Act, which supports the expansion of part-time employment opportunities in the federal service and makes certain changes in the way part-time employees are provided fringe benefits and counted under employment rulings. "Part-time workers," the President stated, "are an important but relatively untapped national resource."

Focus on Part-Time Careers, a counseling service in Seattle, Washington, is determined to change the image of part-time work as generally low paying, low skilled positions. "The average person," says Nancy Inui, president, "is a college graduate interested in a job offering responsibility, growth, and advancement, although not necessarily all three."

Inui counsels those looking for part-time jobs and helps encourage employers to develop part-time positions to replace full-time positions. Since Focus began in 1975, more than five thousand people have been placed in part-time positions.

When you interview for a permanent part-time job, inquire about fringe benefits: sick leave, vacations, and health insurance. Many companies offer full benefits to permanent part-time employees. Employers are recognizing that part-time employees are as committed as those who work full time. They are skilled workers whose productivity is usually very high. A part-time worker with a family is often a good employment risk. The same employee, working full time, might require too much time off. "Two employees handling a forty-hour-a-week work load is a smart way to go," maintain many employers. "It's especially true in a job that may become monotonous on a forty-hour-week basis."

"I look for part-time women workers with families," an official of the city of Alexandria, Virginia, told me recently. "They are my most efficient workers. These women are interested in working when they are in the office. Socializing, coping with family problems, phone calls, and doctors' appointments are all done on their own time. I am paying the women to work; that is exactly what they do, and they do it well. The whole situation is advantageous for everyone."

Job Sharing

Job sharing is a recent and growing trend in today's employment picture. Essentially, it means two people divide one permanent full-time position. Both people share all the responsibilities, hours, salary, and benefits of the job. Job sharing has opened many exciting careers to those who, for a variety of reasons, don't want to work the traditional forty-hour week. For the new mother who wants to maintain her career and be with her child, job sharing is a way to work that should be explored.

Judy Hodges and Carol Parker are the directors of Jobsharers, Inc., a nonprofit resource center dedicated to advancing the recognition and acceptance of job sharing and part-time career employment in the Washington, D.C., metro area.

"Seminars are held for people interested in job sharing," Carol Parker told me in a phone interview. "Subjects include the history, techniques, and application of job sharing; developing a work schedule; dividing job responsibilities; criteria for selecting a partner; advantages to the employer; handling Social Security, taxes, and fringe benefits; convincing the employer; and resources of support. Workshops are also offered on topics such as general interview techniques, successful resume writing, and other aspects of finding a job.

"We are constantly working with employers to develop jobs into job-sharing positions. We maintain a talent bank to help people find partners and keep current job information regarding job sharing and part-time career employment.

"The advantages to the employee are obvious, especially to women who want to be primarily responsible for raising young children. But the advantages to the employer are also great, although the hardest part about job sharing is convincing them of it. To the employer, job sharing means more money in terms of increased production, efficiency, and reduced absenteeism.

"In creative positions, the employer has the advantage of having input from two people rather than one. Two sets of backgrounds, two sets of ideas come much cheaper for him than getting the same talent with two full-time positions.

"Job-sharing clerical positions are also a boon to the employer," continued Carol Parker. "One receptionist can be hired for four hours in the morning and another for four hours in the afternoon. Two typists are more efficient than one who gets weary and winds down near the end of the day."

Carol Parker has found that employers often balk at the job-sharing idea on the grounds that training two people for one job will be an unnecessary expense, but Carol's logic counters that argument: "Such double training can actually become a master selling point. If one member of the team leaves, the remaining partner is there to train the new employee."

Lynette Watts and Sharon Rothman explained how they easily share one social work position. They divide the case load. Lynette works on Monday and Tuesday, Sharon on Thursday and Friday. "We split Wednesday in half, usually overlapping that day for two hours for combined administrative details and discussion."

Jobs can be shared in many different and creative ways. Lucy Johnson, an elementary teacher in northern Virginia, works every morning and her partner works afternoons. Kathleen Borman and her partner, Lois Ginsberg, each teach twenty hours a week, and get together during conferences and office hours. Betsy Kanter and Sue Winters of Indianapolis split their writing/research team as follows: Kathy works nine to one and Sue works from twelve to four. That leaves them an hour of conference time a day. Their boss is pleased because he didn't have to hire a researcher and a writer full time, and either woman can take over the other position in an emergency, "although I could never be the writer that Betsy is," smiled Sue.

People who share jobs believe they do a better job *not* working full time. Lois Ginsberg feels that job sharing makes her a better teacher. She has to prepare half as many lessons as she did previously, so preparation for each lesson is much more thorough. "Besides, I have more time to think about and be creative with my lesson plans. When I was teaching full time, I often used the same plans over and over again each semester."

Flexitime

Flexitime is a system whereby workers choose their own hours of employment. There is a core period of time during which all employees must be present, perhaps from ten to three; otherwise they may choose their comings and goings as long as they add up to the prescribed number of hours each day.

Flexitime is perfect for parents who want to be home to get their children off to school or to a sitter. Or one parent can be home when the children leave, the other when they come home.

Susan and Doug Graham have found the flexitime schedule at their respective jobs opportune for their family life. "I'm home in the morning so I get the children dressed and off to the sitter without a rush," notes Susan. "I work a 10 A.M. until 6 P.M. shift. Doug selected an 8 A.M. to 4 P.M. shift. He picks the children up from the sitter at 4:30, plays with them, starts dinner, etc., and takes care of things until I get home."

A recent study made by the Institute for Behavioral Research, Inc., in Silver Spring, Maryland, evaluated the effects of flexitime in two large federal agencies. It showed that those workers who changed their hours under flexitime increased their time with their children. The data showed a trend for fathers in the change group to be more involved with child care and parent-child activities. The study suggests that even a modest flexitime program can have potentially significant benefits for parents and children in today's busy family lives.

WORKING AT HOME

Many women have developed jobs and careers they can conduct from their home, often gleaned from or based on experience from former full-time jobs. Other mothers have established services and businesses from home by sheer motivation and enthusiasm. Some have explored new careers in writing, business, or the arts that can be effectively accomplished from home offices or studios. Working at home can provide the best of both worlds: time with your children, for yourself, and for your career.

Mara Gold worked as a copywriter for a small Chicago advertising agency when she became pregnant. "I enjoyed my work, but I had no intentions of leaving my baby with a full-time sitter. I had been in charge of certain accounts for several years. I knew them well and liked working with them. The agency cooperated with my postbaby schedule. I go to the office two mornings a week to meet with my creative team; the actual writing and contacts I can do at home as my time allows. We all keep in close phone contact. I can't say if or when I'll go back to a full-time job. Who knows? I may have another baby. I may decide to do strictly free-lance work for more than one agency. All options are open. For the present, being a mother is my primary job."

Pam Vanderwald also convinced her employer that she could work at home after she had her baby.

"I had had three miscarriages. Carrying a baby full term was more important than any job. My doctor nixed full-time work. I was working for the university medical center at the time on a research grant job. I had already worked on the project for a year and had invaluable training. I struck a bargain with my boss to let me work from home during my pregnancy and after I gave birth. The grant lasted only another year. We agreed it was pointless to train someone else as long as I could do the work at home. It gave me an interest throughout my pregnancy and took my mind off my own problems. With the ability to rest more, not commute or stand on my feet, I carried full term, gave birth to a beautiful baby, and followed the project through to its completion."

Dana Leavitt is being groomed to take over her father's surgical supply business and was already involved in executive work when her baby was born. She has arranged to have someone from the office come to her home for a few hours every day. "It's a more efficient way to work. I'm not wasting my time or delegating the baby's care to someone else by going back and forth to the office, etc. My secretary comes at 1:00 every day and stays until 3:30. I organize work in the evening that I want to accomplish the next day. I call in to the office in the morning and ask to have any necessary items brought over. When the baby is older I may consider returning to the office part time. Now, my priorities are here at home. My office personnel is competent and can carry out my directives. I can always work at the office. I cannot always have another chance to enjoy, watch, and guide my baby's development."

Other women have redirected their full-time careers into work at home.

Sandy Marsh, a former full-time math teacher, now tutors high school students in her home. She hires a teenager to amuse her three sons, ages one to five, while she tutors three afternoons a week.

Alene Brown, an architect in San Francisco with a fifteen-month-old daughter, quit her full-time job as a designer and does architectural renderings on a free-lance basis.

Georgia Miller types reports for her ex-boss during ten-month-old Caroline's nap time.

Music teacher Jill Mandel gives voice and piano lessons at home.

Andrea Shiflett, an accountant, does tax work from her kitchen office.

Many have discovered that being at home has stimulated them and gives them time to reach out in new directions and toward new interests.

Janet Langley's art studio went into hibernation to make way for a nursery, so she channeled her talents into textile work. Janet's stuffed and stitched creations line the walls of her sunny Washington apartment. "Textiles were easier to work with once my space was usurped by the baby." Thirteen-month-old Alissa diligently unrolled a nearby ball of yarn. "Of course, there are some drawbacks," she said, eyeing her entwined daughter, "but imagine what she would have done with paint!"

Former second grade teacher Beverly Wilson and commercial artist Phyliss Greenblatt are pooling their talents writing and illustrating a children's book. "So far we have a nice pile of rejections," they laughed. "But we still have a few more publishers to try!"

Kathy Parks and her partner, also former teachers and moms of toddlers, began an employment service for mothers at home; a type of Kelly Girl service. They supply moms with work to do at odd free time during the day. "We realized the endless supply of talent that could be tapped. We have found typists, researchers, editors—so many varied backgrounds. We match our mothers to the work we receive from employers."

Kay Turner and her partner saw a need for a baby-sitting referral service at reasonable rates. "We charge the mother and the sitter a flat fee to register with us, and then supply names to each other."

Working at home is great. Your first rule must be to establish your own space for work on a project that is absolutely childproof, with a lock if necessary. I learned that quickly when Jordan shared my "office" (a desk drawer), while I was on the telephone. Someone I had called during his school time returned my call at 4 P.M. Like a magician doing a sleight of hand trick, those ten fingers unrolled stamps, scattered paper clips, scribbled on manuscript pages, and pulled out the ribbon from my typewriter. That desk and drawer are now absolutely off limits!

It also helps to have your work set up and available to do at a moment's notice as time is available. A separate room is ideal if you can swing it.

Anna Goldstein and her husband moved into a house specifically so that she would have space for a darkroom—a locked room. Developing rolls of film is a lot easier for Anna now than when she had to drag all the chemicals out and set things up in the bathroom after her baby went to sleep. And what could be more dangerous than a forgotten chemical within a toddler's reach?

Architect Alene Brown converted a large double walk-in closet into her office. "When I'm through, I close the door and that's it. We put in a skylight. I hung some plants. It's all the room I need for now. I really didn't have much more room in the cubbyhole at my full-time job!"

Andrea Shiflett's kitchen accounting work is set up on a large rolltop desk that closes and locks when she's through.

There are many ways to work out your space situation. The other aspect to consider is that ever-changing phenomenon—

your child. It's easy to work at home when your child takes two naps a day and plays quietly in his playpen while you write or sketch. But what happens when that cute little bundle starts walking around, tearing up your world? When he gives up his morning nap, you have a nice long stretch in the afternoon. And then, ah ha! Suddenly naps are passé. For me, sending Jordan to nursery school was the answer. Another mother I know hired a sitter to play with her child from nine to one while she worked, although the child was always wise to the fact that mommy was home. Consult Part V for ideas about how to find a proper situation for your child while you work at home.

PART V

WHAT WILL I DO WITH MY CHILD?

14

Part-Time Child Care

Child care is a constant demanding routine that requires frequent breaks. Such breaks have no relationship to your love for your child. I think of such breaks as sanity time. They are essential for me as a person. I have also observed that my attitude toward the children is more positive after I have had time to accomplish something for myself, unencumbered by a baby's feeding schedule, the ins and outs of the car seat, or a toddler's plea for more juice. Whether I choose that sanity time to take a class, shop, or meet a friend for lunch, it is a time solely for me. Sanity time also includes a precious evening out alone with my husband or with friends.

Obviously, you can enjoy free time only if you are able to leave your child with a competent baby-sitter. Few of us could begin to do for ourselves without being able to rely on others to care for our children. Years ago, when families didn't spread out to all ends of the country, the extended family could be depended upon to alleviate many of current child care problems. Today, not only may your child's grandmother or aunt live three thousand miles away, she may also be engaged in a career of her own.

There are a variety of ways you can gain time for yourself on an occasional or regular part-time basis with reliable sitters. When the need arises, full-time day care can also be utilized. All of these options are available if you make the effort to locate them. These full-time situations are discussed in chapter 15.

BABY-SITTERS FOR EVENINGS OUT

A night out with your husband is a necessity. When the time you spend with him is concentrated only on household chores, the baby, and financial problems, signs of stress are bound to show. I have met parents of two-year-olds who have never left their child with a sitter. That is their decision. For me, getting out and seeing people besides the butcher, the baker, or the gossip-maker down the street is an important part of my life. Being away from the routine, alone, with my husband, or with friends, becomes a form of sheer ecstasy.

The first time you leave your newborn may be unsettling because your whole world is tied to this little person. You will probably feel most comfortable the first time you leave your infant if you hire an older woman, experienced with babies, as a sitter. Ask around for the name of someone whom friends use. Choose an evening activity that will get you home for that ten or eleven o'clock feeding—a nearby movie, an early dinner, or a bridge game with friends in the neighborhood. Something short and close that will get you out and establish your routine with a sitter.

We left Jordan for the first time when he was four and a half weeks old. We had theater tickets. Our grandmotherly type of sitter was highly recommended by several friends. She drove herself, for which she charged $1.00, plus a charge of $1.25 per hour (the going rate at the time for teenagers was $.75 in Richmond, Virginia). Jordan was asleep when we left.

He was asleep when I called in at intermission. He was asleep when we got home. The sitter that evening cost $6.00. Next time, with Jordan's sleep habits very reliable, I hired a competent teenager.

Adam, however, was not as easy a baby. He didn't sleep more than two hours at a time until he was eight weeks old. I felt he was a bit difficult for a teenager to handle coupled with his older brother. How I yearned for that older woman during those first few weeks!

Finding a competent teenager to sit can be a major source of aggravation. You'll learn quickly that most mothers guard the names and phone numbers of their sitters as they would a pot of gold. I thought this was selfish and I readily shared my first good sitter with a friend. The result? When I needed a sitter my friend had her booked for weeks in advance.

How do you locate sitters? Ask friends and acquaintances to ask their sitters for names of their friends who baby-sit. Many mothers have second-string sitters whom they use when their regular sitter isn't available. They may share these names with you. When possible, find someone who comes from a large family and has younger siblings. Sometimes these sitters know more about baby care than you do! Don't overlook boys as sitters. When Jordan was ten months old, the thirteen-year-old boy downstairs loved playing with him. Hiring him to sit during evenings was a natural. His parents were usually home in case any problems arose.

If you are new in town, call your local church or synagogue and ask the secretary if she knows of teenagers in your neighborhood who might be interested in baby-sitting. If not, she may give you the name of the youth group leader who might have some names for you. High school employment counselors can also be helpful.

Senior citizen clubs, community organizations, and homes are a good source, too. There are many vigorous men or women who may welcome the time to spend with children and can use supplemental incomes.

When you hire a recommended sitter you'll have a reference.

If the sitter is new, you may want to ask for references. Establish the pay rate when you hire the sitter, not at the end of the evening. Generally, it's not a good policy to let a sitter bring a friend. Never allow a friend of the opposite sex. If you know a sitter and her girlfriend, it may be okay. We have allowed sisters to sit when neither girl wanted to be home alone and both had studying to do.

THE CARE AND FEEDING OF SITTERS

Always write down the number at which you can be reached in bold numerals. (An older sitter can become unnerved and have trouble seeing small numbers without glasses.) Have emergency numbers for police, fire, and poison control close to the phone, and the number of a friend nearby who can be counted on in an emergency. If you're going to a restaurant and the reservation is under another name, be sure to leave that information. Leave a pencil and paper near the phone for messages.

Leave something for the sitter to eat or drink. This need not be elaborate.

Show your sitter how your doors lock and explain any security devices or alarm system you may have, including the smoke alarm. Show the sitter where to find, and how to operate, the television and the thermostat for heat and/or air conditioning.

If your sitter will put the child to bed, leave out pajamas and diapers. Show her the location of the diaper pail and other clothing or supplies. If your child is used to sleeping with a special blanket, pacifier, or friend, be sure to let the sitter know.

Inform your sitter which television programs, if any, your child is allowed to watch. Leave out books with favorite bedtime stories. Show her where the toys are located. Let her know if any areas or food are off limits to her or your child.

Make up a four-ounce bottle of formula for an infant in

case your baby wakes up. If your child takes juice, let the sitter know whether it should be offered in a bottle or a cup.

When you plan to leave, be honest with your child. Don't sneak out. Tell your older child in advance that you are going out and when you'll be back. With an infant you might feel better if he is asleep when you leave. Be warned. This practice can have drawbacks when a baby is around six to eight months old. He may be frightened when you suddenly leave him with a sitter who previously only watched him sleep. You may be wiser to let the sitter put him to bed from the beginning so he is at least used to her face and voice.

You may want to have your sitter arrive fifteen to twenty minutes before you plan to go out. This will enable your child to get used to her and get involved with some type of play so that when you're ready to go you can leave swiftly. Prolonging your departure to the strains of a child's screams will only make things harder on everyone. Jordan often cries when the sitter arrives. We put him firmly in the sitter's arms, give him a kiss, and go. We wait outside the door and listen to how long he keeps it up—the crying usually lasts about thirty seconds. We then leave with a clear conscience.

Add your own sitter dos and don'ts to this list. It will be complete and easy to remember if your next baby requires the same solutions.

MOTHER'S MORNING OUT PROGRAMS

Many churches and YWCAs have programs called mother's mornings out. These programs are drop-in services specifically for mothers of infants and preschoolers. Rates at this writing are about $1 an hour per child; often a reduced rate is offered for a second child.

Drop-in centers usually consist of a large room filled with toys for most preschoolers, cribs for infants, tables and chairs, and a changing table. The number of sitters per child varies at each center, depending on the number of infants in the group.

When you research and discover a morning out center, your first step should be to stop in and observe. Is the place clean? Are there enough sitters to handle the number of children? Do they provide a snack or do you have to send one with the child? Do the sitters seem interested in the children's needs? Do they change dirty diapers? Are the crib sheets clean? Do you notice any hazards in the room?

Remember, morning out services are strictly for baby-sitting; don't expect anything more. You are most interested in a clean, safe, fun, and loving environment in which your child can spend a few hours a week.

I found a mother's morning out program for Jordan when he was fourteen months old. I began taking him for the two-hour minimum (by that time he had given up his morning nap). In the beginning he often cried. Before I left I found a toy that intrigued him and made sure he was involved with some kind of play. As he became used to the situation, I increased the time I left him. When he was twenty months old, I left him from 9:30 to 1:00. He couldn't wait to go. He loved the toys, the children, the activity. He was almost indifferent when I arrived to take him home. As the same children were there every week, he talked about his friends and looked forward to seeing them. He even babbled on about the "babies"—those still in cribs, some as young as three months, which was the minimum allowed at the center.

Consider the bonus of even one day a week at such a program. Your child learns to interact with other children and become sociable. You have the morning off to shop, take a class, sew; but the afternoon becomes free time, too, during nap time. Having one day a week that you can depend on for yourself can do wonders for your mental health and your relationship with your child.

CLASSES WITH SITTER SERVICES

Many racquet ball clubs, tennis clubs, YMCAs, and county recreation departments offer activities with sitter services available. Most facilities are well equipped, similar to those in mother's morning out programs with toys and cribs. However, I have seen some sitter services in which the children and the sitter are virtually alone in an empty room. The children are expected to bring their own toys.

I took Jazzercize and aerobic dance classes offered through the county recreation department. Classes were held in a local church and the church nursery was used for baby-sitting, so there were plenty of toys for the children. Each class was only forty-five minutes long, so it was a good way to ease Jordan into a group sitter situation. The room was bright and sunny, the sitter cheerful and full of smiles; the children warmed up to her immediately. Initially, Jordan cried when I left him, but the sitter assured me the crocodile tears lasted about two minutes; as soon as he became involved in an activity he was fine.

Similar classes were located closer to home. Though they would have been more convenient, I felt the quality and continuity of the sitter situation was most important at the time. The same children and mothers were involved for almost a year. The classes and the sitting services were great diversions for both of us.

When you enroll in classes with sitter services, investigate the facilities before you sign up. Ask for names of other people who have used them. One bad situation can be traumatic for a youngster and, in turn, make life more difficult for you. Be aggressive in expecting certain services. True, you need them. But they need you, too. If they don't do their jobs well, they won't have a job. If something doesn't look right, you might want to bring it to the attention of the program director.

AFTERNOON BREATHERS

Do you feel the need for relief from your child in the late afternoon? Consider hiring a preteenager to take your baby out for a walk in the stroller or just to play with your child while you do other things. When we moved from Washington, I sorely missed the brother and sister team downstairs, aged nine and ten and a half, who loved to take Jordan out to play after school. For this, they were thrilled to receive 50¢ an hour. He adored them, and they felt like big shots taking care of him. By 3:30 or 4:00, my low-energy time of the day, especially when I was pregnant, I was glad to have a free hour to read a few articles in a current news magazine, start dinner, or just relax.

These youngsters were able to wear Jordan out a lot better than I could. He was always ready for dinner and early bedtime after an afternoon with one of them. And I was always home and available in case of any problems. In bad weather they played with him in the house. Noisy? Sometimes. But happy noise. And it usually canceled out the five o'clock arsenic hour!

BABY-SITTING COOPERATIVES

A baby-sitting cooperative is made up of a group of families who sit for each other's children on a point basis. There is no money involved. Each family receives points for baby-sitting and subtracts points when another family sits for their children. Co-ops are an ingenious way to save money on baby-sitting, providing you have the time, disposition, and inclination to sit for other people's children.

Setting up a Co-op

The following is a guideline for a relatively small group of families (twenty to thirty). If your co-op continues to grow, more rules and regulations may need to be added, but you can expand on this basic idea.

Leadership

Leadership of the co-op should be fulfilled by a president or coordinator and a secretary. The president conducts meetings and deals with problems. The secretary keeps track of points for all members. (The secretary position may be rotated on a one- or two-month basis.) If both of these positions are permanent, office holders may be paid in sitting time.

Operating Rules

1. Members arrange all sits themselves after checking with the secretary regarding who is available or who is most in debt of sits. The secretary will establish a time when calls can be made to her.
2. A member may refuse to sit without giving a reason.
3. Members are responsible for canceling a sitter twenty-four hours in advance or may arrange a replacement, or pay for a sitter out of pocket if cancellation is made less than twenty-four hours ahead.
4. Members must accept their fair share of sitting jobs.
5. Members must write out specific instructions for sitters regarding feeding times, nap schedules, special friends, bed-time.
6. All members should sign a statement releasing each other from liability in case of injury to a child.
7. A limit of member children under one roof at any one time is established by the co-op.
8. Sits are usually in the sitter's home. More points are paid if the sitter goes to the member's home.
9. Each member must pay a nominal fee to be established to cover photocopy and mailing costs where applicable.

Record Keeping

1. Two sets of records are kept: one by the member and one by the secretary.
2. Each member informs the secretary of times when he/she absolutely cannot sit due to classes, car pools, etc., to eliminate unproductive calls by the secretary.
3. The members' goal is to maintain as close to zero points as possible.

4. A member gains points by sitting, subtracts points when using another member as a sitter.
5. Points are figured by an established number of points per hour. Time is rounded off to the nearest half hour. Additional points are charged for each child over the first.
6. A limit of a certain number of points can be established against any member.
7. Extra points are earned for:
   a. weekend sitting
   b. sitting in someone else's home
   c. sitting after midnight
   d. sitting on holidays

New Members

1. A new member must be sponsored by an existing member.
2. Sponsoring member must hold a coffee to introduce the new member to the group.

Departing Member

If a member quits, she must pay off any debt at a rate set by the co-op.

PLAY GROUPS

Play groups offer an excellent way to have free time while maintaining involvement with your child's social development. Play groups usually consist of three to five mothers and their children, all about the same age. Each mother takes a turn watching all the children in her home, while the other mothers have time for themselves.

Play groups can begin at any age. My friend Davida describes her daughter Erica's early play group. "We started the group when Erica was five months old. In the beginning it was purely baby-sitting—two mothers watching four children and playing a game of musical cribs.

"The children began to interact when they were about eighteen months old. Then it was rather wild. Most mornings were a free-for-all, each child taking toys away from another. When the kids reached two, we instituted more structure. We developed activities: arts and crafts, singing, and story time, along with free playtime. We went on nature walks, picnicked in various places within walking distance."

Davida explained that the play group began with only one afternoon scheduled for each week. When the children gave up morning naps, it was changed to two mornings a week. The play group met at a different house each week. During nice weather they met completely outside.

"At eighteen months," she continued, "we began to give the children lunch. It seemed the kids always ate more at play group than at home! And the days we were off, we didn't have to make lunch. What a pleasure!"

Finding mothers with children of your children's age is not always easy. If you live in a friendly community of apartments or townhouses, you might readily spot prospects. If you live in a house, scout at playgrounds in local parks and during walks around your neighborhood at different times of the day. Ask friends and family if they know of women your age with similarly aged children who might want to become involved in a play group. You may meet other interested and interesting moms through religious or service organizations.

Establishing a Play Group

If you would like to start a play group, here's a plan for establishing and running a group smoothly.

Plan Play Group Policies

When you gather a group of mothers eager to participate, one planning session is necessary to establish guidelines. Depending on the ages of the children, free play may be all that the children are capable of, or specific arts and crafts and other projects for older children. Here are some of the aspects for which you will have to establish guidelines:

- Health policies (Some groups allow colds, nix diarrhea.)
- Discipline
- Types of snacks
- Diaper and potty policies
- Vacation and holiday rules
- Sick days
- Trading

The regulations should be typed and copied so each person knows the policies.

Start Everyone Comfortably

Plan an outing with moms and tots so everyone will get to know each other. A picnic at a park is always fun, or simply a get-together for play and refreshments. Some play groups meet for two or three weeks, everyone together, before the moms begin to leave. Anticipate lots of crying at first and be honest with each other about how the children react.

Be Prepared

The day the play group meets at your house, be prepared. Make sure you have snacks. Take out the toys you want the children to play with. Close rooms that are off limits to the children. Put away that special toy of your child's. It will be hard enough for your child to adjust to sharing his mom and his toys with others; don't contribute to any further stress. And don't be surprised if your child is the most obnoxious when the play group meets at your house.

Play groups can meet at a library story hour, at the zoo, or for any special activity that may be in town for the week. They don't always have to meet in someone's home.

When everything runs smoothly, play groups are a marvelous way for your child to meet and interact with other children of his own age. It's fun for you to participate in this development and wonderful to have free time while feeling secure about leaving your child in the care of friends.

THE NURSERY SCHOOL DECISION

Many parents struggle with the decision about whether or not to send a child to nursery school. It's hard to decide what is best for a child, particularly a first one. Somewhere between the child's second and third year, many mothers confront the question of whether or not their child (and the mother) could benefit from a nursery school program.

I've spoken with mothers who express a range of attitudes from enthusiastic "pro" to emphatic "no!" Some felt it was the perfect need for one child but not another.

Usually, those mothers who are in favor of nursery schools mentioned such advantages as "it helped my child relate to other children," "prepared her better for school," "added to his development and awareness," "gave me free time regularly," "made a second pregnancy easier"—the list is endless.

On the negative side, reactions are, "Children go to school so long; who needs a few more years of nursery school tacked on?" or, "For what it costs and what goes on, I can certainly do the same things at home."

Parents should make the nursery school decision based on the maturity of their child; the time, space, and patience the mother or father must expend in doing projects with their child; and the number of children of the same age he or she comes in contact with on a daily basis. Finances and available nursery school facilities are, of course, paramount considerations.

For us, the choice was clear. There were no children Jordan's age in our apartment complex. All the friends I had made who had children Jordan's age had dispersed in various directions after our first year in Washington. Jordan was twenty-three months old, and I was quite concerned about his social development. He was an eager learner and needed more than just mother's morning out and class sitter services. I personally do not enjoy daily sessions of finger painting, play dough, and other assorted nursery projects. Our apartment was small and after a few days of messy-type play added to the usual disorder, I balked. I concluded that if someone else was more patient and creative in these areas than I, he was better off learning from that person. In addition, the child craved the constant stimulation that a nursery school could offer and I could not.

The result? I enrolled Jordan in nursery school shortly after his second birthday for two mornings a week from 9:30 to 12:00. He loved it. He even asked to go to school on non-school days. When I contracted to write this book, I increased the sessions to three mornings a week. The teacher observed that the added continuity was more beneficial to Jordan, and I've always been grateful for her patience and contribution to his development.

There are various types of nursery schools, each with its own philosophy and structure. Some are religion oriented, learning oriented, work oriented, or strictly play. Most important is that you visit and observe several schools with varying philosophies until you find one that you feel is right for your child. The following section suggests points to look for in a good nursery school and provides a discussion on the different types of schools generally available. All may not be available in every area.

Evaluating Nursery Schools

How can you locate a good nursery school? Ask friends or relatives with nursery-aged children which schools their children attend. Ask those with primary school children for their references. You'll learn which ones are good and which to stay away from. If you do not have such a resource, begin with the yellow pages of your phone book under schools—Nursery and

Kindergarten. Make a list of the schools on a sheet of paper and leave space for notes. Then call each school and ask to speak to the director.

First, ask about the school's philosophy. Don't be specific; let the director respond. If your question is met with, "What do you mean by philosophy?" then you can assume the school has no set goals. Eliminate.

Ask about student-teacher ratio; any more than eight to one may be questionable, especially in a program for two-year-olds in which the recommended maximum should be a seven-to-one ratio. A seven-to-one ratio is fine if the class limit is fourteen, but a seven-to-one ratio with twenty-one children in a class is unrealistic. It may consist of one teacher and two aides. One school director I called was incensed when I suggested their twelve to one ratio was questionable for three-year-olds. What happens when a child needs help in the bathroom? Is the class left unattended?

Ask about facilities, fees, and variety of programs. If you need extended day care, ask whether these facilities are available after the regular morning program concludes.

Determine the accessibility of the school to your home and whether or not pick-up service is available if you don't have a car.

By asking these few questions over the phone, you can eliminate many schools and save yourself chase-around time and effort. When you narrow down the three or four schools you may be interested in, make an appointment with the director and spend a morning observing. You may or may not wish to bring your child. You might like to stay around after the session and talk with other mothers about the school and its program.

The Philosophy

You probably will have determined the school's basic philosophy on the phone. You want to know how much actual learning and structure are stressed, or whether the school focuses on a general play situation. How much teacher involvement is evident? Are the children free to learn on their own, or are they expected to do what everyone else in the class is doing? Is there a total emphasis on learning? Is learning done through play, or is play gently guided but unstructured? If there is a religious orientation, does its philosophy agree with yours?

The Physical Layout

The actual nursery room should be bright and cheerful. Look through some of these guidelines and compare them with the schools you visit.

Is the environment safe, pleasant, stimulating, clean?

Is there a variety of space for different types of play (art, cooking, reading and puzzles, dress-up, blocks, sand and water table)? Is the space adequate for each activity?

Are there sturdy toys and materials that help children learn through play?

Are play materials reachable and easy to use?

Are there indoor and outdoor facilities for large-muscle exercise?

The Program

Here is a typical morning program in a quality nursery school (from the *Children's Learning Center Parents Beginning of the Year Handbook,* Rockville, Maryland).

Opening

A happy feeling to be carried through the day is initiated at this time. The children are welcomed to the class, the flag is saluted, a favorite song is sung, the class and teacher formulate the plans for the day, and perhaps a learning concept is introduced.

Worktime or Self Selection Time

The children are free to choose from many different activities in the room. The activities include the special art activity of the day, painting, clay, crayons, blocks, riding toys, playhouse, language arts center, science center, math center, library, etc. The teachers are always present at this time to guide, teach, and help the children learn to make decisions.

Clean-up

The children are encouraged to participate positively and actively in clean-up time. Responsibility and independence are stressed especially at this time.

Snack Time

A healthful, nutritious snack is served, followed by clean-up.

Group Time

The class is called together for a planned language arts, science, social studies, or music lesson. The lessons are introduced through a fun approach (playing a game, learning a song, dramatizing a flannel board story, etc.).

Outdoor Time

The children have ample space for use with riding toys and to run and exercise their large muscles. During inclement weather, the multipurpose room is set up with large-muscle indoor play equipment.

Special Teacher Time

The children have an opportunity to meet regularly with the music and creative dramatics teacher, dance instructor, and physical education instructor.

As you observe a morning in a nursery school program, watch for the following.

What determines the flow of activities? Time schedule? Teacher? Child interest?

Does the program seem too structured or too loose?

Is there sufficient variety and change of pace?

Are children required to do as everyone else does, or are they free to explore on their own if they prefer?

The Teacher

A bright enthusiastic teacher can make even the most dismal atmosphere come alive.

What is the teacher's background? He or she should hold a degree in early childhood education.

Do the teachers seem happy and enthusiastic?

Do the teachers, or teacher and aide, work well together?

How do the teachers talk to and interact with the children?

How are behavior problems handled?

The Children

Do the children seem happy and stimulated?

How do the children interact with each other? With the teacher?

General Policies

What licensing has the school obtained?

What is the tuition? How are payments made? Monthly? Quarterly? Are there special rates for more than one child?

What are the school's emergency procedures?

What are policies on diapers? (Some schools allow two-year-olds in diapers. They will change wet ones but you must be on call for dirty ones!)

Does the school have adequate insurance coverage?

Are snacks provided by the school, or are they the parents' responsibility on a rotating basis?

During field trips, how will your child be transported? What are the safety standards of these trips?

Parent Involvement

Are parent-teacher conferences planned throughout the year?

Are parents welcome to visit and observe at any time?

What are the channels for communicating with the teachers?

How Nursery Schools Differ

Generally, nursery schools are operated for either learn-through-play or total-play situations, with paid teachers, or teacher and aide, hired by the director. Here are some diverse situations.

Cooperative Preschools

If you are concerned about your child's adjustment to school, or *your* adjustment to leaving him, perhaps you should consider a cooperative nursery school. A co-op school is owned by the parents. Parents hire the teacher. Philosophy and structure are determined by the parents. Parents work as teacher's aides, which may include floor sweeping, potty duty, and nose wiping. The advantage of a co-op school is that you observe how your child learns and relates to others. You'll also learn how professionals handle common problems.

If your child has separation problems, a co-op school is a good way to ease him into a social school situation. He'll know the days his mom is the teacher's aide and also the days his friends' moms are aides. Fathers, grandparents, aunts, and uncles often participate in the program if they care for the child regularly during the day. Often a full-time baby-sitter may be involved.

Some mothers complain that they are often involved more than they would like to be. They emphasize the importance of establishing how much parent involvement is expected.

On the positive side, most parents of co-op preschoolers feel they make special friendships within the group. Often parent education lectures, discussion groups, family outings, and get-togethers are organized by a special committee of parents.

Directors of many cooperative preschool programs whom I interviewed stressed a most important aspect: each school is autonomous. Do not evaluate cooperative schools as a whole; rather, consider each school independently.

Montessori Schools

The Montessori method of preschool education was developed by Maria Montessori in Italy during the early 1900s. One of the basic differences in a Montessori classroom is the role of the directress. Based on the theory that a child must learn by doing, the Montessori teacher becomes a sensitive observer who is ready to help, but only when needed. Montessori teachers should be trained in the method, which uses specially designed materials to prepare children for the world around them.

You can best get an idea of the Montessori program by observing and comparing and talking to the directors. Although the method should be similar, each school may differ in its approach to carrying out the method.

15

Full-time Child Care

DAY CARE IN YOUR HOME

If you want to return to a career or must work shortly after a baby's birth, you will have to become your own personnel department. Just as your company seeks and hires competent help, you will now become an employer, and a very discriminating one. You must hire someone who will raise your child while you are gone, a person who can detect all the nuances of your infant's well-being as if she were the mother.

Ideally, the best but most costly full-time care for your child's first year is a woman who comes to your home, cares for your child, and may do light housekeeping. This person must meet the requirements you establish for the job—reliable, self-sufficient, hard-working, friendly, and loving. She should be expected to respect your method of child raising and be thoroughly cognizant of the importance of her role in the development of a human being.

How do you go about finding such a person? In the same way any employer seeks an employee—through ads, agencies, and references from others.

Advertise for a full-time baby-sitter in a reliable newspaper. When people respond, be businesslike and assertive. Know what the job is worth and establish a salary, vacation policies, days off, etc.

Call baby-sitting services and ask about the sitters they provide. You will pay top wages for women recommended by such services and should expect highly qualified people.

If you are interested in part-time child care on a regular basis, a good source is the student employment office of your local college. You may be able to hire a student who schedules all of his or her classes in either the afternoon or the morning and can work for you in large blocks of time. A student whose classes are on Monday, Wednesday, and Friday may be available on Tuesday and Thursday. I know several couples who provide a room for a college student to live in all semester in exchange for sitting and child care during specific times of the week. One mother works three mornings and the student takes over. This student also sits during evenings when needed.

Community organizations for older people can often put you in touch with an adult who may enjoy taking care of your child a few days a week.

Before you hire anyone, insist on references. Always double-check the references with a personal phone call. You can learn much more about a person by asking a few adroit questions than you'll ever get in a letter. (A person will give only references that are likely to be favorable.) If the reference is far away, make the long-distance call; it's a nominal investment in your child's well-being.

One valuable procedure for judging someone's competence for your job is to have her work in the house with you for a day or two on a trial basis. She will be on her best behavior, but it will give you the opportunity to observe how she reacts to your child, to you, and to your home. Introduce her to your child's routine, where everything is, how you run things. It will be faster and easier for all than if you were to leave her with only a list of instructions on her first day. You may be uneasy having her underfoot, but it's worth starting everyone out comfortably. It will also give the employee time to decide whether she wants the job. It's frustrating to break in someone, go to work, and have her leave the following week.

After you hire a woman to care for your child, establish a list of checkpoints. You know when your child naps, so it might not be unreasonable for a sitter to be on the phone at that time. Call once or twice during the day, or have friends or relatives call. If the phone is constantly busy, be suspicious. You are not paying someone to spend the day making personal phone calls. Ask neighbors to drop in occasionally to make sure the woman isn't spending her day in front of the television. If you have made arrangements for her to do light housework, be reasonable in the amount that you expect her to do—enough to keep her busy, but not so much that she will neglect your child, feel she's asked to do too much, and quit.

Another concern is that the unsupervised housekeeper might do what's easiest for her rather than for the well-being of your child. Persistent diaper rash on an infant's bottom will indicate that diapers are not changed often enough. Parking a toddler in front of the television all day or stuffing her with junk food is probably not your idea of great care. You must be a detective. If TV is not on your "do" list and your child knows how to operate the set, find the programs, and sing advertising jingles, you should be suspicious. If she asks for lollipops on a regular basis when they are usually forbidden in your household, you don't need Sherlock Holmes to form your own conclusions.

In the course of time any number of anticipated or unforeseen problems may occur when child care is turned over to another person. The one that is voiced most frequently by parents I interviewed is the concern for the child's social development. As the child matures, he needs social interaction with other children. Your sitter may walk the baby in a stroller, play with him at the playground, but will not be a total surrogate mother who invites other children home to play with your child. This is something the parents must consider doing on weekends.

Whatever decisions you make in hiring full-time child care, *never* hire someone out of desperation. If you have to delay returning to work, do so. Finding a reliable person who will stay is a number one priority. A series of employees can be detrimental to your child's care and development. It can also create a problem with your job if you frequently take time off to find replacements.

As in any employment relationship, to keep your employee happy you may want to offer her slightly more than the going rate, with automatic pay increases built in. Pay her for holidays. Give her a bonus at Christmas and a gift for her birthday. Treat your help as you would be expected to be treated by your employer. You must establish the price to be paid for the well-being of your child and your peace of mind.

FAMILY DAY CARE

Licensed family day care usually consists of one woman giving care to children in her home. This kind of care is best suited for infants and children of ages two and under.

A family day care giver is usually not trained in any way, but should be a warm loving person who enjoys children. Her licensed home means that it has been inspected and approved by the health department as a safe, healthy environment.

Family day care centers are often advertised in the classified section of your newspaper under child care or baby-sitting services. Or call your county department of social services and ask if they have a listing of licensed homes.

Begin your selection process with a few hours of observation. If the caretaker balks or treats you as a nuisance, cross her off your list immediately. Here are some of the points to observe:

—Ratio of children to care giver. Four to one should be the maximum.

—Safety hazards. Check things that should generally be child-proofed, such as caps on electrical outlets, heavy objects that could be pulled down by a small child, sharp objects left to a child's reach.
—Number and condition of toys
—Clean nap areas
—Nutritious snacks and meals. You may want to ask for a sample of the week's menu.
—Observe the way the care giver relates to the children. While you're there, she should be devoting more attention to the children than to impressing you, unless you're asking specific questions.
—Are the children happy together? Are they clean, or do they appear in need of a diaper change and a face wash?
—Are infants cared for lovingly, or are they shoved into a corner while more attention is given to older children? As this will be one of an infant's first attachments besides yourself, it is extremely important that a loving atmosphere be maintained.
—Are the children taken outside? Is there outdoor play equipment or a park nearby?
—Does the care giver take the children on her errands to the grocery store, etc.? (I know of one woman who takes her charges everywhere she goes. Not only are the children not in car seats, but they aren't buckled in and usually stand up and hang over the seats. I don't think I would be comfortable not knowing where my child is at all times and would probably suffer apoplexy if I found out my child was being transported in the above manner!)
—Does the care giver read and play with the children, or is the TV a major source of entertainment?
—What are her policies regarding vacations? Illness? Emergencies?

Many family day care situations are not licensed, but consist of a mother with an infant or toddler who is home anyway and is interested in caring for one or two more children of the same age as her child. The best way to evaluate this situation is to spend a day or two with the mother and child to determine how she relates to her own child and to yours. You'll be able to discuss philosophies about child rearing and see whether her parenting policies agree with yours. By spending time with her you'll be able to evaluate how she runs the home, what her family relations are, and what her interest is in your child. To many children this situation is the warmest and most loving, as long as you have confidence in your decision and the person who will care for your child.

DAY CARE CENTERS

Day care. What is your reaction to those words? Do you think of ragamuffin, unloved children walking around with empty expressions? An institution? Possibly; many are. But high-quality, well-run day care centers are springing up everywhere as a response to many mothers of preschoolers entering the work force. Quality centers offer more than basic custodial care; these have a wide range of activities for all preschoolers.

Notice that I stress the word *quality*. That characterizes the only kind of center to which you should entrust your child. Observe the center in the morning when the children are active. Visit several centers before choosing the one you feel is best for your child. This may take time, but it is a minute investment compared to the major time your child will spend there during his most formative years. Ask to spend time in all the rooms in which your child would be throughout the day. Then use this guide as a checklist to see how each center stacks up.

General Policies

What licensing has the center obtained?

What are the center's hours? Does this schedule coordinate with yours?

Is the location convenient?

What is the tuition? How does it fit into your budget? Are there special rates for more than one child?

Does the center have access to a doctor, psychiatrist, social worker, or speech pathologist?

What are the center's emergency procedures?

Does the center have adequate insurance coverage?

Will the child be permitted to try out the center for a specified time before you sign him up for a full term?

If the child is unhappy or becomes ill, what is the refund policy?

Staff

Are the teachers trained in early childhood development?

What is the child-teacher ratio? Some guidelines offered by the Montgomery County, Maryland, Community Coordinated Child Care Council follow.

Age	*Child/Adult Ratio*	*Group Size*
Under two years	two to one	Family care recommended
Two years	four to one	Family care preferred: if center is used, no more than eight in a group
Three years	five to one	Fifteen maximum
Four to five years	seven to one	Eighteen to twenty maximum

Do the teachers seem happy and enthusiastic?

Do the teachers work well together?

How do the teachers talk to and interact with the children?

How are behavior problems handled?

Do the teachers have breaks from classroom activities?

Does the teaching staff remain fairly stable? What is the turnover rate for aides, volunteers, and substitutes?

Program

How is the day structured?

A Typical Day

7:00–7:30—Opening, breakfast and free play.
8:30—Organized play; child may choose from arts and crafts activities, cooking, etc.
10:00—Nutritious snack. Good health habits discussed. New foods introduced. Table manners stressed.
After snack—Circle time with story, games, songs, drama, large-muscle activity, indoors or out, depending on weather.
12:00—Lunch program.
1:00–3:00—Nap time. Each child has his own cot, pillow, blanket, along with special friend.
3:00—Informal wake-up and snack.
3:30–6:00—Less structured recreational activities.

What determines the flow of activities: Time schedule? Teacher? Child interest?

How are transitions between activities accomplished?

Does the program seem too structured or too loose?

How varied are the activities and experiences to which your child will be exposed?

Is there sufficient variety and change of pace?

How is rest period or nap time handled?

Environment, Equipment, and Activities

Is the environment safe, pleasant, stimulating, clean?

Is there a variety of spaces for different types of play (art, cooking, reading and puzzles, fine motor activities, dress-up)?

Is the space adequate for each activity?

Are there sturdy toys and materials that help children learn through play?

Are play materials reachable and easy to use?

Is there safe, sturdy equipment for large-muscle activity, indoors and out?

Are the children given adequate time to explore a variety of activities on their own as well as in a group?

Are quiet times interspersed with activity?

Snacks and Mealtime

Are snacks nutritious or sugar-laden junk food?

Is a variety of food offered during the week?

Does lunch consist of a protein food, at least one vegetable, a starch, a wholesome drink, fruit or an occasional dessert?

Are creative food experiences and good manners part of the daily activities?

The Children

Do the children seem happy, comfortable, stimulated?

Do they interact with each other?

How do the children react to the teacher?

Are the children clean? Do they look taken care of?

Parent Involvement

Is there close communication between parents and care givers?

Are parents welcome to visit and observe at any time?

Are there opportunities for parent involvement through advisory boards, family activities, policy councils?

Are parent-teacher conferences planned throughout the year?

A quality day care center should strive to be an extension of the family rather than a baby-sitting or custodial service. Its goal should be to strengthen rather than replace the family by involving parents, staff, and children with the center. The center should aid the child by helping him to develop a positive self-image and to get along with others.

PART VI
HAVING FUN!

16

Weekends that Work

Ah, the weekends. Time for recreation, family, fun, friends. When Monday arrives you feel refreshed, revived, ready for a new week.

If that doesn't describe you, don't be dismayed. A first baby tosses a monkey wrench into the recreation pattern of every couple. Many discover that weekends result in a *weakened* condition. If weekends tend to be a concentrated dose of your weekly schedule and are wearing you out, it's time for a new approach.

MAKE WEEKENDS A CHANGE OF PACE

Establish a weekend pattern that spells change of pace, a change from your weekly schedule. When you were working, Saturdays and Sundays were for different activities than the daily grind. No reason to change that now. There are certain recurring routines that have to be accomplished no matter what day of the week it is, such as eating, changing diapers, or a last-minute laundry load, but these can easily be incorporated into creative weekend planning.

It's up to you to make a complete weekend change by planning it! Your husband has a routine break by being home and away from his job. He may be content to putter around the house. You do that all week. If you want a real change, *you* have to make the effort.

Examine some of your past weekends. If they all seem to be a blur, a panorama of sameness, note the symptoms. It's time to treat the condition. For the next few weeks jot down your weekend activities. What do you find? Did you take the baby to the park or for a walk in the neighborhood? To the grocery store? That's what you do all week. Watch for these types of activities. Suggest that your husband take the baby for a walk and swing ride while you do something else (besides cleaning up the kitchen). Maybe you'll all enjoy an afternoon at the park together once in a while, but you'll know it was a mistake on Monday when you go for a stroll with your usual destination—the park.

Make weekends a time to explore new places, have new experiences, with your family, or just the two of you. Consult your Friday paper for weekend happenings. If you have a museum in your city, look into their programs. A planetarium or an observatory is a fun trip. Architectural walking tours can be taken with a baby in a backpack. House and garden tours are a fascinating diversion and a good source of decorating ideas.

Your county or city recreation department might sponsor bicycle tours or nature walks. Both activities can be done with your child in a carrier. Check special-interest clubs for their programs. Art councils schedule exhibits, openings, and lectures. Preplan for a new activity each week, or at *least* once a month. It will be something to look forward to and to talk about afterward.

WHAT'S SO GREAT ABOUT SATURDAY NIGHT?

In trying to decipher the weekend doldrums dilemma, I asked a group of mothers in suburban Chicago, "What are the pitfalls of your weekends? How do you avoid them and improve your time?"

Carolyn, the mother of a nine-month-old, made a comment that was surprising to many of us. "Often, I hate going out on a Saturday night." This caused a few raised eyebrows until she continued. "By the time I feed the baby, give her a bath, put her in her pajamas, get her to go to sleep, take a shower, and get myself dressed, I'm ready to crawl into bed. I couldn't care less about spending a night out on the town!"

There were some cries of, "I know how that feels" among the group, until Enid, whose son Eric is almost two, offered a suggestion. "Rearrange your schedule when you're going out. I take a shower and wash my hair earlier in the afternoon, during Eric's nap time. It's much more enjoyable to soak in the tub, do my nails, when I'm not rushed. I pick up the sitter early, before Eric is ready to go to bed, and let her put him in his pajamas, read to him, and get him to bed. If he doesn't get a bath that night, it won't kill him. By going out earlier, we avoid that horrible half hour of trying to get him to bed, and somehow he never gives the sitter the hard time he gives us about going to sleep."

"Have you ever tried 'decadence'?" I suggested. "It's a marvelous alternative to Saturday night stress. Decadence means hiring a sitter in the middle of the afternoon and doing something that is usually a real nuisance with Jordan along. We have taken in Saturday matinees at the theater, gone to museums, had picnic lunches with a bottle of wine, a loaf of french bread and cheeses (it's amazing how decadent picnics can be without peanut butter sandwiches and apple juice). Once we rented horses and spent an hour on a trail ride. Jordan usually naps in the afternoon anyway!

"When decadence is pursued during the day, we try to carry

it over to the evenings. We don't go out at night; rather, we spend the evening over a leisurely dinner at home. We find a new gourmet meal to try and prepare it together. The ultimate decadence to a meal at home is putting the baby to bed, showering, donning a long dress for me (usually out of style, but sexy enough for home) and a nice pair of slacks and shirt for Richard. We have cooked flaming steaks, sipped good wine, added candlelight, and soft music, of course. Beef fondue is fun, too—long, languishing, relaxing. We leave the dishes to soak until morning; there are more romantic things to do after the evening scene has been set!"

"Sometimes our budget doesn't allow for baby-sitters," added another woman. "We make our weekends enjoyable without going out. In nice weather we plan outdoor activities during the day, perhaps make an easy dinner, and relax in the evenings. Saturday nights often are a push with restaurant reservations, rushing, picking up and dropping off baby-sitters. Not to mention the expense. It kills us to splurge on a nice restaurant meal with results less than the gourmet extravaganza we had expected. Often, we'd rather go to bed early and take a leisurely trip on Sunday."

THOSE POSTBABY CHANGES

"How has your form of weekend entertainment changed since you've had a child?" I asked several groups of mothers.

"We gave up movies quickly! With the cost of a sitter added to the price of a movie these days, we think three times before rushing to see something that didn't get rave reviews!"

"We put in cable TV. We can see six movies at home for the cost of one movie out. We save the expenses of a sitter and gas, and the popcorn we make at home is better; cheaper too!"

Other weekend changes after having children were mentioned.

"I must be with adults part of the weekend. I make it a point to have friends over or meet with them every weekend."

"I make an effort to go out with friends who don't have children, so I don't lapse into baby conversations."

"We entertain more at home than we did before the baby was born. Not involved dinner parties. We may invite one couple over for dessert and to play bridge. Once we pulled out our old Monopoly game; it's amazing how vicious that can become. Or four-person Scrabble—a killer!"

Suggestions of Ping-Pong, pool, poker, and Rummy-Q came out in the discussions. One mother said she and her husband have a passion for electronic games. "There's always something new on the market to tempt us."

Weekend dos and don'ts were also voiced.

"Getting together on weekends with friends who had small children was fun when the weather was nice and we met outdoors. But a Sunday afternoon in someone's apartment with a few toddlers fighting over toys was a disaster. Now we spell each other one weekend a month. One couple takes the other's children and gives the other couple an afternoon or a full day free."

"We loved trying new restaurants. Give us a recommendation and we were out the door. Not anymore. We tried to take Kevin with us to a nice place once. Never again. It's unfair to expect a child to sit through a leisurely dinner. There's too much temptation in a nice restaurant: silverware to bang, water to spill, tablecloths to pull, and sugar to rip open. Avoid this at all costs. Kevin is best at a fast food restaurant in a high chair where he can macerate a hamburger and drop food on the floor without anyone giving us dirty looks."

"Have you noticed how quickly things change with children? One month you can take a child somewhere; the next month it's a disaster. The first year we could take Danny almost anywhere in the backpack or a stroller. Once he began to walk, he wanted his freedom. No backpack. No stroller. In the summer we picnicked and let him run in wide open spaces. In the fall we picked apples and took walks in the woods. In the cold weather we found the indoor shopping malls. Next?"

WEEKEND MEAL PLANNING AND ENTERTAINING

The conversation frequently turned to weekend meal planning and entertaining. Many of the moms came away from the brainstorming discussions with marvelous new ideas.

Keep weekend meals simple: hamburgers on the grill, cold cuts, take-out food.

Make a fairly elaborate meal on Friday night, resulting in leftovers to use over the entire weekend: chicken, gelatin molds, and various salads and vegetables can complement sandwiches and cheeses all weekend.

Plan weekend meals on Wednesday evening, and do your big shopping on Thursday. Use Thursday food ads and plan ahead so you don't have to run out for supplies during the weekend.

Think of entertaining as an art form and make it fun for you. Not just work. Barbecues, fondue, and lasagna are a few simple, easy-to-prepare meals that can look elegant with the addition of candlesticks, coordinated paper place mats and napkins, and an improvised centerpiece.

Most of the mothers agreed that the most fun about entertaining is getting together for a relaxing evening with good friends. The food is almost secondary. Don't knock yourself out trying to impress people with elaborate food preparation. Your evening won't be enjoyable. You really entertain for your pleasure, don't you? We were more impressed with a casual beer, bread, and beans party than with a gourmet French dinner when the hostess hardly sat down. The peasant fare was so uniquely served that one hardly noticed it was only chili.

Sunday brunches can be successful, especially for beating winter Sunday doldrums. Try these ideas.

A lox and bagels breakfast with a fruit salad and donuts for dessert. All the makings can be purchased and prepared that morning.

Make a quiche the night before and reheat.

Soak thick-sliced french bread in a batter laced with a little orange liqueur for a different French toast treat.

Appoint your husband the Omelet King and have him do the major part of the work.

Other suggestions to simplify entertaining are described below.

Start a gourmet club! Each menu is planned and hosted by a different couple. One part of each meal is allocated to the other guests. No one person ever does all of the work, and everyone helps with the clean-up.

Make a good roast and dress up the meal with an interesting salad or vegetable. Serve buffet; it's a lot easier.

If you don't have a dining room table and are opposed to serving guests in the kitchen, have a few couples over and use bamboo lap trays. No table to set, and the guests clear up after themselves.

Use paper plates and napkins. They have such terrific-looking ones these days, who needs to be bothered with doing dishes?

When you do go to the effort and have a large party, cook dishes ahead and freeze as much as you can. Planning and shopping takes the most time. Make organized lists. Shop without your child so you won't forget anything and can make rational substitutions when the store is out of the exact ingredient you need.

Schedule the party for after your child is asleep, and you won't have to interrupt your entertaining for stories, etc. Or, if your entertaining must be earlier, hire a sitter to take care of your child while you're busy. Leave the baby with a friend or your mother for the evening.

Consider using your baby-sitter efficiently after your child is asleep. Many love to make extra money by helping to serve, clear tables, and do the dishes so you can be with your guests. It's so nice not to have to tackle a sink of dishes when the party is over.

Use a catering service or order some precooked items from a caterer or local deli. No need to slave over a hot stove if you don't have to.

Most important when entertaining: Have fun! Enjoy!

17

Traveling/Vacations

The Bahamas, Jamaica, Hawaii, Europe, Aspen—what a thrill to plan an exciting vacation. Then along crawls that ball of mischief who eagerly, innocently rips up your travel brochures and shatters your dreams. What are you going to do with your vacation time now that you have a baby?

There are only two obvious alternatives, both filled with apprehension: leave the baby home or take him along.

VACATIONS WITHOUT YOUR CHILDREN—FINDING CARE

Each one of us dreams of a few days away, alone with our husbands, no one to care for at 6:30 in the morning, no crying, no fussing, no toys to clean up. Bliss. Just like the old days. But how can you leave that sweet adorable baby? That child that depends so much on you? That child only you know how to care for?

Easily.

Make up your mind that your sanity, often your relationship with your husband, may depend on a break from your child and your routine. Your child can survive for a few days without you. If he's not fed exactly as you feed him, if his nap is a half hour later, if his face remains a little dirtier, and his shirt and pants aren't well coordinated, your child will grow up in spite of it. Adopting this attitude doesn't mean you love your baby less.

A vacation without the baby, whether it's overnight or a fortnight, can make you feel better about yourself. When you and your husband take time to renew your relationship, your parenting is bound to be optimal. The minute you start feeling guilty or have any qualms, you won't have a good time. Worse still, you won't go.

Feeling comfortable about leaving your child lies in the confidence you have in the person with whom you leave your child. If the baby's grandparents are willing, able, and live nearby, they are the most obvious choice. Sisters, aunts, or other capable members of your family may also be willing to take on the responsibility.

There are baby-sitting agencies that specialize in overnight child care. Look these up in both the white and yellow pages under child care, nursing care, or baby-sitting services. These agencies refer mature women who are licensed to do this kind of work. Each woman has references and is checked out thoroughly by the agency. Prices range differently in each city, from a low of $20 per twenty-four hours to a high of $50 per twenty-four hours at this writing.

You can also find overnight sitters through personal recommendations from friends. A baby nurse you used when you came home from the hospital may be a likely choice. Often, a regular housekeeper will agree to stay. If you can afford a sitter for only two nights, take those two nights and make the most of them. Even one night on a weekend can make all the difference in the world. If it will make you feel more comfortable, have a neighbor or friend stop by or call to make sure everything is all right.

Another way to leave your child is to trade child care responsibilities with friends. You watch their children for a few days while they in turn take care of yours. Try it for a weekend first. If it works on both sides, you're in good shape to go for a week. If the children are of the same age and get along well, they'll play together, amuse each other, and generally require less supervision on your part. The only added work will be in dressing the children in the morning and getting them to bed at night. Grocery shopping and errands will be difficult with more children, so plan ahead and get everything done before the onslaught.

Trading works best when you know the family well with whom you are swapping and are comfortable with the way the parents handle their child. If your parents live in different cities, and you can't afford live-in sitters, trading is the only way you'll be able to vacation without your child.

VACATIONS/TRAVELING WITH YOUR CHILDREN

Many parents can't take advantage of any of the above procedures for vacations and must take the child along. Family vacations can be a lot of fun if they are thought out well and planned carefully.

The ABCs of Travel

Automobile Travel

Car travel is probably the way people travel most often with small children. It can be long and tedious. However, we have had positive results on long car trips with our son, Jordan. When I say positive, everything is relative. It is not a great pleasure no matter what you do. I never propose that anything is really easy with a child. But to the extent that a child from the ages of six months to three years can be good on a seven-hundred-mile car trip, he is.

The important factor in car travel is to have all supplies together and accessible when you need them. Presumably, your child will be in the back in a car seat. If you are in the front passenger seat, you will be reaching back and spending much of the trip with your derriere pointed toward oncoming traffic. The solution? The nondriver can sit in back with the child. On our first trips Jordan would sleep and be content by himself during morning travel, but after lunch one of us would sit in the back seat and entertain him. (I recall reading *Curious George* to him twenty-four times during a traffic back-up!)

We used a small plastic foam cooler to preserve the food supplies: juice, cookies, lunch, and fruit. We also kept cups, utensils, napkins, and wipes behind the passenger seat within easy reach. A separate tote bag held diapers, wipes (put into plastic Ziploc bags to keep them moist) and a change of clothing, along with his blanket. A third bag held toys and books. Keeping things in their own place makes it easy to grab what you need and dispense it as efficiently as confined space and motion will allow.

Make sure you stop and take short breaks midmorning and at lunchtime. Plan to be at your destination by late afternoon, before the five o'clock cranky period hits its zenith and in ample time to find a place to eat and sleep.

If you are staying in a motel, most have portable cribs available free of charge. They never have bumper pads, however. If you want this protection for your child, it pays to buy an inexpensive set of pads for traveling. Don't be surprised if your child won't sleep in this crib; it's a strange environment and the child's schedule has been thrown off. It's also hard to leave the room and let him cry himself to sleep. Often, it's more expedient for you and your husband to go to bed early and either let him sleep with you for the night or let him fall asleep with you and transfer him to the crib later. Many of the bedtime rules followed at home may have to be suspended while traveling.

Air Travel

Take advantage of air travel while your child is young.

Children under age two fly for free, and most airlines are quite accommodating to families with young children.

Each airline company has different amenities for babies and young children. All will try to seat families first and leave an empty seat next to you if possible. They all will warm bottles and heat baby food. You can easily get milk and orange juice on the plane. Hamburgers, hot dogs, and peanut butter and jelly sandwiches are available for ticketed children over age two if requested with reservations.

When making your reservations, ask the airline what facilities they have for small children. Always try to reserve the bulkhead seat. It's the first row of seats behind first class and the storage area. These seats usually offer more room for your child and a bit of space, depending on the plane, for the child to walk around. It is also a more private area if you are nursing. On coast-to-coast flights with movies, the screen is often behind that row of seats and is less desirable for the other passengers. If you are flying during off hours, often most of the seats in that row are unwanted and you can have them all to yourself. When the movie goes on and the lights go off, it's bedtime!

The larger airlines offer the most amenities to young children. United has a marvelous bassinet for children up to seven months old. There are two bolts in front of the bulkhead seat, to which this boxlike frame bed attaches securely. You can put your infant into it, zip her up, and be relatively relaxed during your trip. On United, always reserve the bassinet seat.

American Airlines has a car seat for children up to age two that you can strap your child into for safety. Request one when making your reservations.

TWA has a small cardboard bassinet for an infant so you can lay him on the seat next to you.

Eastern airlines provides meals to unticketed children under age two who are eating table foods. Request a meal with your reservations.

Travel lightly. Take one convenient tote bag for all of your supplies: diapers, wipes, a lap pad or cloth diaper for changing, an extra change of clothing, snacks in Ziploc bags, toys, books, etc. Bring as few toys as you can, selecting them carefully for maximum interest time. Don't forget that favorite stuffed animal, blanket, or pacifier. (Something for your child to suck on during take-off and landing is imperative.) One toy that worked well for me on a cross-country flight was a handful of Colorforms that fit into my wallet. (Colorforms are bright vinyl shapes of delightful characters such as the Peanuts gang and various super-heroes.) We decorated the plane window again and again—good for at least twenty minutes. The stewardesses usually have small diversions like cards, puzzles, balloons, and games for older children.

Some mothers prefer taking evening flights, hoping their children will sleep. One rule I always follow on a flight, however, is to order a glass of wine for *me*. Somehow, things never seem quite so bad no matter how many passengers ask to change seats!

Train Travel

If you haven't been on a train in a while, train travel has changed. The new Amtrak trains are a pleasure. They have seats comparable to those found in first-class airplane sections; clean, roomy washrooms; and attractive lounge areas. If you book overnight sleeping passage, the bunk beds have a protective webbing around them to keep children and infants from falling out. There are children's menus in the dining cars, observation decks for diversion, and ample room to run around. I have found train travel especially convenient on trips that Jordan and I have taken by ourselves when I have chosen not to drive.

Trips to Try—Making Them Work

We've examined many modes of travel, but *where* do you take a vacation that all of you can enjoy?

A common complaint from many mothers is that family

vacations are often a break for everyone but the mother. She still has to worry about feeding and caring for the child, but in unfamiliar circumstances. One mother said that the only time she gets a vacation is when they visit her parents; then her mother cooks, cleans, and takes care of her and her family!

Naturally, when you take a family vacation, everyone has to eat and be cared for. Don't dwell on the negative aspects of vacationing with the kids. Concentrate on the positive—having a great time—and you will!

Ski Trips

Many ski resorts have day care facilities for your children, depending on their ages. Often they are for toilet-trained children over age two and a half. We took two ski trips with Jordan, once when he was six months old, and again when he was nineteen months. We chose places that specifically offered day care facilities for him. When he was six months old we were able to leave him with a woman recommended by the ski association who watched children in her home. It worked out well. We dropped Jordan off in the mornings and skied until three. Then we picked him up, played with him, fed him and put him to sleep. At 7:30 we used a recommended babysitter and went out to dinner.

The following year Jordan was nineteen months old, so we selected a different resort that had a day care center at the foot of the slopes. It was an excellent facility and reasonably priced. One woman was assigned to care for every three children. They had nap facilities and provided hot meals. Jordan loved it, and at the end of the day he didn't realize we had walked in to pick him up!

That year we rented a condominium rather than a hotel room—a charming one-bedroom with a loft. There was a grocery store nearby, so we could eat in, put the baby to bed in a separate room, and have a leisurely evening in front of the fireplace. Cooking didn't bother me. We were always so bushed from skiing all day and too tired to go out to a restaurant, although sitters were available. Having breakfast at home was easier, too. It was quicker and less expensive than sitting through overpriced restaurant breakfasts.

I will admit that there were drawbacks to that trip. We were tired at the end of a day of skiing. All we felt like doing when we got back to our room was sitting peacefully in front of the fireplace and relaxing. But Jordan wanted attention, needed feeding, bathing, and had to be put to bed. My husband pitched in willingly and did his share and more. But Jordan had difficulty adjusting. We had trouble getting him to bed in the new surroundings and he woke up in the middle of every night.

In retrospect, we know we would have enjoyed the trip more without him, but we had no choice. We had just moved to a new area and knew no one. Both sets of grandparents lived across the country. Our minimal vacation budget did not include a baby-sitter. Everything about this trip was less than optimal. Still, we got away, we improved our skiing, we had lovely afternoons together, and we fell in love with Vermont. If we hadn't been willing to compromise, improvise, and plan the vacation, we could have stayed home and done nothing. We would have missed all the positive aspects of the trip. We made up our minds it would be great, and we made it that way as best we could.

Summer Resorts

Many summer resorts welcome small children and cater to them. Facilities are usually for children over age two. Programs range from playground supervision to camp facilities with arts and crafts, swimming, and nature studies, to a youth hotel with overnight dormitories for children aged three to eighteen. Most are staffed with college-aged counselors.

Camping Trips

Camping trips are a fun family way to get out together and enjoy nature. There's so much to show children at any age.

The key to success is in the planning. Spend an evening rehearsing what a trip with your child will be like. Plan for the mishaps: rain, cold weather, cuts and bruises. Make a complete inventory of everything you'll need and have it all together ready to go into the car the night before or the next morning. Pack so that the things you will need first are easy to reach. Plan your food supplies carefully; premix pancake batter and spices in Ziploc bags. Plan, plan, plan—from the sugar in your coffee to the amount of firewood you'll need.

Try a one-night test run ahead of time to see how things work out before you attempt an extended trip. If you and your husband were enthusiastic campers before you had your child, a bit of modification will be necessary. Small babies are easy to take on camping trips. You can hike with them in back-packs or chest carriers and let them sleep in a portable crib or playpen if your tent is large enough. When children begin to toddle around, setting up camp, cooking, and cleaning are long ordeals for them to sit through with little attention. Yet these chores are part of the *gestalt* of camping. Start campfires early; you may be better off cooking on your stove than over a fire. Keep your meals simple, limiting them to those that will take very little time to cook. Be prepared to have your chores take about twice as long as usual because you'll need time out to play with your child. Involve him in what you're doing. Find a simple task like collecting sticks, stones, or leaves, or give him a shovel and show him a pile of dirt. Keep him busy with something you deem important and you'll be able to accomplish more in less time.

Anticipate trouble in convincing a toddler that the vast tent with its sleeping bags rolled out is a place to sleep, not to do acrobatics. Consider going to sleep early with your child. A feeling of security, a little quiet time, and the fresh air will knock him out quickly. Make sure you bring a pair of waterproof boots for the morning dew if your child is walking.

Many parents of toddlers recommend camping with other

families in the same situation. Children have playmates, adults have companionship, and chores are accomplished with less effort. And it's always fun to share your adventures!

Beach Vacations

Trips to the beach or a lake were by far hailed as the most successful family vacations by those interviewed. Renting a beach house or condominium on the water won the "best vacation" vote. A few chose motels. Beach vacations worked well because they were relaxing and all could enjoy themselves. Infants were placed in playpens under beach umbrellas while mother or father could sun and swim. Toddlers enjoyed playing in the sand, throwing beachballs, and jumping waves with their parents. Nap times and evenings allowed husbands and wives relaxing, unhurried time together.

"My husband and I loved playing with Todd on the beach. Of course, neither of us could just sunbathe and vegetate; one of us had to have our eye on the baby at all times. But, you know, lazing in the sun seemed like such a bore when you could really have fun with your family."

Mothers who rented beach houses or condos never complained about the cooking, because that was about all the responsibility they really had. Things were kept easy and dinners were often eaten out. There was no house to clean, no errands to run, no laundry to do, so the cooking seemed like nothing! And what's so tough about toasting English muffins for breakfast and making sandwiches for lunch?

Whenever you take a vacation, research the various ways and places to go. Make sure your plans are designed for the enjoyment of everyone, especially yourself. For example, you might bow out of a fishing trip that will be great for your husband but leaves you on the shore taking care of the children. When everyone has a memorable time, your family vacations will be something you'll treasure always.

PART VII
ANOTHER BABY?

18

And Now We Are Four . . . or More

You've done it: you're pregnant again. (Was it that memorable weekend?) Here are some ideas for getting through this time.

OH, THOSE SECOND PREGNANCIES!

In talks with mothers, the attitude that prevailed was that a second pregnancy is certainly different from the first one. With the first, you could rest undisturbed, sleep late on the weekends, pamper yourself. You had only you to take care of.

Who can forget the first few months of pregnancy? Sleep becomes an addiction that can't be satisfied. If your first child takes an afternoon nap during this time, you know where you will be—in bed! Forget everything else. Take advantage of the time to nap. It was my luck, of course, that Jordan gave up naps and I conceived simultaneously. By two o'clock in the afternoon I would be crawling toward the bed and he would start to dance. I did something I swore I would never do; I turned on the television cartoons. They saved my life. Ten-minute cat naps were better than none. I also learned to doze while he jumped all over me—an invaluable trick after our second child was born.

Nausea may be harder to handle the second time around, too. You have to prepare food for your first child no matter what it does to your stomach. I think the first four months of my second pregnancy were spent with my head close to the commode.

Second pregnancies do seem to pass faster; you're too busy with your first child to notice every ache and pain, to consider which layette items to buy, whether to buy a foam or inner-spring crib mattress, or whether to use disposable or cloth diapers. In fact, you may find yourself surprisingly unprepared emotionally for the coming of number two because you didn't spend nine months thinking about every detail of the baby's arrival.

If your first child is old enough to understand the pending change in the status quo, begin early to read her books about new babies. We particularly liked the *Berenstain Bears' New Baby*. Today, however, if I mention that book to my husband, he will get a wild look in his eyes and begin to act crazed. Maybe we started *too* soon??

Sign up for a refresher LaMaze class if you took LaMaze previously. It consists of one or two classes that stress the breathing techniques. It's also a good way to meet others having second babies around your due date.

I hope that you are more prepared for the birth of your second child than I was. We had moved across the country from Silver Spring, Maryland, to Albuquerque, New Mexico, two weeks before. We had no furniture due to a truckers' strike and the superinefficiency of the movers. We bought new mattresses that were on the floor. Richard had just started his new job. It was his fourth day, and my water broke three and a half weeks early. To say I was unprepared was an understatement.

We had been practicing LaMaze but hadn't reviewed pushing (that was scheduled for the next week). I didn't have a bag packed, because I didn't have much with me to pack. All of my nursing bras, nightgowns, baby's clothes, blankets—you name it—were packed neatly in a drawer in a dresser in a warehouse in Maryland. We had no crib. Nothing. I had seen the new doctor once; luckily he was the one on call. But the baby came so fast I really wouldn't have cared who it was, as long as someone was there. All of this didn't matter really, because Adam Mark was born, healthy and beautiful.

I loved my hospital stay. It was one of the first times in three years that I felt I had achieved peace. If my bottom hadn't hurt so much, it might have been Nirvana. I opted for a private room since it was only $6 a day more than a semiprivate room—certainly the best $18 I ever spent in my life. I slept, relaxed, wrote letters, read, nursed and cuddled my baby. I had only one visitor, since I knew no one in Albuquerque at the time. At first I thought it would be depressing, but found visiting hours the best time for sitz baths and showers. The total lack of responsibility was marvelous. The interruptions were a joy; my new little boy whom I looked forward to seeing every feeding—my best, my sweetest company.

Take advantage of this time; you may not find such precious moments for a while.

Your hospital may allow toddler visits. Welcome your toddler but, please, limit his stay. I suggest a half hour as the absolute maximum. I balked when the hospital requested only a ten-minute visit, but after Jordan had jumped on my sore tummy, sent my bed up and down and in various positions the manufacturer hadn't thought of, screamed and yelled, wanted a bracelet like my hospital band, and other delights—I knew they were right. He stayed for an hour. I was exhausted for the rest of the day.

If you have maternity insurance, take full advantage of its benefits and don't be in a rush to leave the hospital. If you really feel poorly, stay an extra day. It can be false economy to go home and face your other child and home responsibilities when you are only marginally up to it.

POSTPARTUM HELP

If you don't have insurance, come home as soon as you can and consider hiring a baby nurse. The charge of $50 or more per day may seem high, but compared to the daily hospital charge the cost is a bargain.

When you get home, it is imperative that you have someone to help you. The problem this time around is not the new baby. His care seems almost minimal, but the care of your first child may wear you out. (Naturally, the younger your first, the more care he will require.) It takes all your energy to lift, feed, change, and bathe a newborn, but your toddler can run you ragged and demand extra attention. Those extra trips to the refrigerator for apple juice or milk may be more than your stitches can handle. Use your time with your toddler wisely: read stories, color or introduce art projects that can be accomplished while you relax or stretch out on the bed.

If you can ask your mom, a relative, or a friend to help you, you're lucky. If not, hire your regular sitter to come by after school to play with your toddler and relieve you. If it's summer, have her spend the day, or perhaps only the afternoon. For a little extra, she might straighten up the house, help fold the laundry, or do any of the hundreds of things that need to be done. Maybe there is a teenager who drives in the neighborhood and can run errands, pick up groceries, or whatever. The more you enlist the aid of other people, the faster you will recuperate. Neighbors will usually be happy to help, too.

A second child can be a frustration as well as a delight. Being an old hand at mothering, you probably figured that the new baby would be a snap—very little work compared to your active toddler. How quickly we forget! You may have to reread those chapters in your baby books on how to calm a crying baby or how to get a baby on a decent feeding schedule. Perhaps with the first you had all sorts of ideas on when to pick up the baby when she cried, how long to let her cry, etc. Now, with your second, you may pick her up on the first squeak so as not to wake your other child, or because it eliminates half the noise level in your house. Or you may wince as you let her cry while your older child needs help at the potty in the middle of a feeding.

You'll definitely be amazed at the differences between children. Your first may have been a sleeper, but your second doesn't seem to know what that word means. Your first may have been active; the second, a quieter baby.

I think the hardest aspect of this time was how tired I constantly felt. Jordan napped often as a baby, so I could lie down when he did. With Adam, the minute he fell asleep, Jordan needed attention and all visions of a nap to offset those nightly feedings vanished quickly. I threatened to buy stock in under-eye makeup; I used it in quantity to cover up those deep dark circles!

Certainly, you won't have the time to concern yourself with all that you did with your first baby. As the weeks pass, you'll have to fit the baby into the family's schedule, rather than you to his. While your older child may have had the advantage of napping in his crib at the hours he set, your second may find his naps taken in his car seat while you car pool your older child to nursery school, gymnastics, or play groups. Time is a luxury; that's why it's necessary to carve out some of your day for you.

You may be frustrated trying to coordinate everyone to fit your schedule. I thought I had everything planned. Jordan would be in school every morning and Adam would sleep, so I could work on the book. For the first three months, Adam decided that the most he would sleep on any given morning would be twenty minutes. The faintest noise from my typewriter must have seemed like an explosion to him. My hands got stiff from writing longhand every morning. You'd laugh if you saw my setup. Adam would be in the carriage in front of the couch. I had one foot on the carriage, rocking it while I wrote furiously on a pad in my lap. On other days Adam would be awake in the baby swing while I was at the typewriter. I'd type away, take two minutes out for some cooing to make him happy, and then go back to the manuscript. Between the noise of that baby swing and the noise from my typewriter, I swore one of us would end up with permanent brain damage. Now, at four months of age, with the book in first draft, he takes a fairly reliable one-hour morning nap. Who knows how long that will last?

19

Epilogue

I will admit I was apprehensive about having a second child. But it is a joy to have a baby in the house again. There's nothing like those first smiles, that clean smell of a baby after a bath, the warmth of the small body, the wonder and awe the experience brings.

Friends who recently had first babies are boggled at my routine. How do I get the baby nursed and organized, send Jordan off to nursery school, and work on the manuscript every morning? I am by no means a superwoman. I am extremely content for the first time in years. I'm realizing a new satisfaction from being a mother. Jordan, at three, is a delightful companion. He loves his new brother. I think the three-year age difference was perfect for them. When I nurse Adam, Jordan lifts up his shirt and nurses his favorite friend, Lamby. Luckily, Jordan notes, Lamby doesn't spit up like Adam does.

Happiness, joy, and pleasure do stem from day-to-day

living. I am involved in personal growth and the growth of two beautiful boys. After years of moving and feeling unsettled, we are finally becoming part of a community in a very exciting area. Albuquerque is the type of place we have always looked for.

A few years ago I would have thought the big thirty-year birthday mark meant I was over the hill. Today, I feel I'm just beginning a slow ascent to the summit. It's a marvelous time of my life—a marvelous time to be a woman, a person, a mother in the 1980s. Never before have women been so alive, so aware, so feeling, so fulfilled. I hope that you can enjoy these years with me, wherever you are. Isn't life great?!!

Appendix

INFORMATION ON MOTHERS' SUPPORT GROUPS

International Childbirth Education Association, Inc.
P.O. Box 20852
Milwaukee, WI 53220

RESOURCE MATERIAL FOR CAREERS, SELF-GUIDANCE

Catalyst
14 East 60th St.
New York, NY 10022

Catalyst provides career information and self-guidance material for women. Informative brochure, bibliography list, case history profiles list. Also has listings of women's centers throughout the country.

VOLUNTEER INFORMATION

National Center for Voluntary Action
1214 16th St. N.W.
Washington, DC 20036

BACK TO SCHOOL

Project on the Status and Education of Women
Association of American Colleges
1818 R St. N.W.
Washington, DC 20009

Write for publications list.

NEW WAYS TO WORK

New Ways to Work Publications
457 Kingsley Ave.
Palo Alto, CA 94303

Publications list on job sharing.

National Council for Alternative Work Patterns
1925 K St. N.W.
Suite 308a
Washington, DC 20006

Interesting newsletter for members regarding alternative work patterns.

U.S. Department of Labor
Employment Standards Administration
Women's Bureau
Washington, DC 20210

Variety of publications on women workers in the United States.

CHILD CARE

Superintendent of Documents
U.S. Government Printing Office
Washington, DC 20402

Write for publications list on child care and baby-sitting.

Selected Bibliography

PART I: DISCOVERING YOU! A PERSON *AND* A MOTHER

Chapter 1: A New Outlook on Motherhood

Baber, Virginia, and Skaggs, Merrill Maguire. *The Mother Person*. Indianapolis, Indiana: Bobbs-Merrill, 1975.

Kelly, Marguerite, and Parsons, Elia. *The Mother's Almanac*. Garden City, N.Y.: Doubleday Co., Inc., 1975.

McBride, Angela Barron. *The Growth and Development of Mothers*. New York: Perennial Library; Harper and Row, 1973.

Radl, Shirley L. *How To Be a Mother and a Person Too*. New York: Rawson, Wade, Inc., 1979.

Chapter 2: The Postpartum Rainbow

Boston Women's Health Collective. *Our Bodies, Ourselves*. New York: Simon and Schuster, 1971, 1973.

Cardozo, Arlene Rossen. *Women at Home*. New York: Doubleday & Co., 1976.

Delliquadri, Lyn D., and Breckenridge, Kati. *Mother Care*. New York: Pocket Books, 1979.

De Rosis, Helen A., M.D., and Pellegrino, Victoria Y. *The Book of Hope; How Women Can Overcome Depression*. New York: Bantam Books, 1976.

Rakowitz, Elly, and Rubin, Gloria S. *Living with Your New Baby: A Post-Partum Guide for Mothers and Fathers*. New York: Franklin Watts, Inc., 1978.

Reed, Constance, with Stone, Robert B., Ph.D. *How to Be Beautiful After the Baby Comes*. New York: Franklin Watts, Inc., 1979.

Rozdilsky, Mary Lou, and Banet, Barbara. *What Now? A Handbook for New Parents*. New York: Charles Scribner's Sons, 1972, 1975.

Feeling Great

Arpel, Adrien. *Adrien Arpel's 3 Week Crash Makeover Shapeover*. New York: Wallaby.

Dahlena. *The Art of Bellydancing*. New York: Bantam Books, 1975.

Folan, Lilias H. *Lilias, Yoga and You*. New York: Bantam Books, 1976.

Hittleman, Richard. *Richard Hittleman's 30 Day Yoga Meditation Plan*. New York: Bantam Books, 1978.

Meilach, Dona Z. *How to Relieve Your Aching Back*. New York: Bantam Books, 1979.

Misset, Judi Sheppard. *Jazzercise*. New York: Bantam Books, 1978.

Sassoon, Beverly, and Sassoon, Vidal. *A Year of Beauty and Health*. New York: Fireside, Simon and Schuster, 1979.

PART II: HOW DO I FIND TIME?

Castle, Sue. *The Complete Guide to Preparing Baby Foods at Home*. New York: Doubleday & Co., 1973.

Fanning, Tony, and Fanning, Robbie. *Get It All Done and Still Be Human.* Radnor, Pa.: Chilton, 1979.

Lakein, Alan. *How to Get Control of Your Time and Your Life.* New York: New American Library, 1974.

Lansky, Vicky. *Feed Me, I'm Yours.* Wayzata, Minn.: Meadowbrook Press, 1974.

Moore, Alma C. *How to Clean Everything.* New York: Simon and Schuster, 1971.

Pinkham, Mary Ellen, and Higgenbotham, Pearl. *Mary Ellen's Best of Helpful Hints.* New York: Warner/B. Lansky Books, 1979.

Winston, Stephanie. *Getting Organized.* New York: Warner/B. Lansky Books, 1979.

PART III: WHAT DO I WANT TO DO?

Bolles, Richard Nelson. *What Color Is Your Parachute? A Practical Manual for Job Hunters and Career Changers.* Berkeley, Calif.: Ten Speed Press, 1979 (revised annually).

Dyer, Dr. Wayne. *Your Erroneous Zones.* Chicago: Funk and Wagnalls, 1976.

Fanning, Tony, and Fanning, Robbie. *Get It All Done and Still Be Human.* New York: Chilton Press, 1979.

Goodman, Ellen. *Turning Points. How People Change Through Crisis and Commitment.* New York: Doubleday, 1979.

Lakein, Alan. *How to Get Control of Your Time and Your Life.* New York: New American Library, 1974.

PART IV: WHAT ARE MY OPTIONS?

Chapter 12: Back to School?

Barron's Handbook of Junior and Community College Financial Aid. Woodbury, N.Y.: Barron's Educational Series, Inc., 1979.

Blaze, Wayne, et al. *Guide to Alternative Colleges and Universities.* Boston: Beacon Press, 1974.

Lenz, Elinor, and Schaevitz, Marjorie Hansen. *So You Want to Go Back to School. Facing the Realities of Reentry.* New York: McGraw-Hill, 1977.

Tobias, Shiela. *Overcoming Math Anxiety.* New York: Norton, 1978.

Chapter 13: Back to Work?

Albrecht, Margaret. *A Complete Guide for the Working Mother.* New York: Award Books, 1970.

Curley, Jayne, et al. *The Balancing Act—A Career and a Baby.* Chicago: Chicago Review Press, 1976.

Curtis, Jean. *A Guide For Working Mothers.* New York: Touchstone, 1975.

Greenberg, Barbara Kay, with Schaeffer, Louis A., M.D. *Help! A Handbook for Working Mothers.* New York: Thomas Y. Crowell, 1978.

Hewitt, Geof. *Working for Yourself: How to Be Successfully Self-Employed.* Emmanus, Pa.: Rodale Press, 1977.

Laurey, Jean Ray. *The Creative Woman's Getting-It-All-Together at Home Handbook.* New York: Van Nostrand Rheinhold, 1978.

Loring, Rosalind K., and Otto, Herbert. *New Life Options—The Working Woman's Resource Book.* New York: McGraw-Hill, 1976.

Meier, Gretl S. *Job Sharing.* W.E. Upjohn Institute for Employment Research, 1979.

Norris, Gloria, and Miller, JoAnn. *The Working Mother's Complete Handbook.* New York: A Sunrise Book, E.P. Dutton, 1979.

Schwartz, Felice N.; Schifter, Margaret H.; and Gillotti, Susan S. *How to Go to Work When Your Husband Is Against It, Your Children Aren't Old Enough, and There's Nothing You Can Do Anyhow.* New York: Simon and Schuster, 1972.

PART V: WHAT WILL I DO WITH MY CHILD?

Curtis, Jean. *Parent's Guide to Nursery Schools.* New York: Random House, 1971.

Collins, Alice H., and Watson, Eunice L. *Family Day Care.* Boston: Beacon Press, 1976.

Evans, E. Belle, and Saia, George E. *Day Care for Infants.* Boston: Beacon Press, 1973.

Lowndes, Marion. *A Manual for Baby-Sitters.* New York: Little, Brown, 1975.

Orem, R.C., ed. *Montessori, Her Methods and the Movement.* New York: G.P. Putnam's Sons, 1974.

Steinfels, Margaret O'Brien. *Who's Minding the Children? The History and Politics of Day Care in America.* New York: Simon and Schuster, 1973.

Winn, Marie, and Porcher, Mary Ann. *The Playgroup Book.* New York: Macmillan, 1967.

PART VII: ANOTHER BABY?

Berenstain, Jan, and Berenstain, Stan. *The Berenstain Bear's New Baby.* New York: Random House, 1974.

GENERAL PARENTING BOOKS

Boston Women's Health Book Collective. *Ourselves and Our Children.* New York: Random House, 1978.

Brazelton, T. Berry. *Infants and Mothers.* New York: Delacorte, 1969.

Brazelton, T. Berry. *Toddlers and Parents.* New York: Delacorte, 1974.

Caplan, Frank, ed. *The First Twelve Months of Life.* New York: Grosset and Dunlap, 1973.

Dodson, Fitzhugh. *How to Parent.* Los Angeles: Nash Publishing, 1971.

Dodson, Fitzhugh. *How to Father.* Los Angeles: Nash Publishing, 1974.

Frailberg, Selma H. *The Magic Years.* New York: Lyceum Edition, Scribner's, 1968.

Ginott, Hiam G. *Between Parent and Child.* New York: Avon, 1969.

Princeton Center for Infancy and Early Childhood. *Parents' Yellow Pages.* Garden City, N.Y.: Anchor Press, 1978.

Smith, Helen Wheeler. *Survival Handbook for Preschool Mothers.* Chicago: Follett, 1978.

Spock, Benjamin. *Baby and Child Care.* New York: Pocket Books, 1976.

Index

G

H

I

J

L

M

N

O

P

Q

S

T

V

W